Stylistic Criticism and the African Novel

Stylistic Criticism
and the African Novel

▼▼▼▼▼▼▼▼▼▼▼▼▼▼▼▼▼▼▼▼▼▼▼▼▼▼▼▼▼▼▼

A Study of the Language, Art and Content of African Fiction

Emmanuel Ngara

formerly Senior Lecturer in English,
National University of Lesotho

LONDON
HEINEMANN
IBADAN NAIROBI

Heinemann Educational Books Ltd
22 Bedford Square, London WC1B 3HH
PMB 5205, Ibadan · PO Box 45314, Nairobi

EDINBURGH   MELBOURNE   AUCKLAND
HONG KONG   SINGAPORE   KUALA LUMPUR
NEW DELHI   KINGSTON   PORT OF SPAIN

Heinemann Educational Books Inc.
4 Front Street, Exeter, New Hampshire 03833, USA

British Library Cataloguing in Publication Data

Ngara, Emmanuel
    Stylistic criticism and the African novel.—
    (Studies in African Literature)
    1. African fiction (English) – History and
    criticism
    I. Title   II. Series
    823   PR9344

    ISBN 0-435-91720-X

Set in 10pt Times by Mid-County Press, London SW15
Printed in Great Britain by Biddles Ltd., Guildford, Surrey

Contents

Preface

▼▼▼

A large portion of this book is based on the lectures I gave to students who took the course we entitled 'The African Writer and the English Language' at the National University of Lesotho. The aim of the course was to examine African writers' handling of the English language in relation to aesthetic and socio-political issues raised by contemporary African writing, with special reference to the novel. Some of my views on the authors discussed in this volume were clarified and modified as a result of student participation in the course. I should therefore acknowledge my debt to all my students for whatever contribution they may have made. In particular I wish to mention the following students who wrote very stimulating and illuminating essays: Jacob Mokhoane, Lineo Letsie, Lucy Sefika and Lindiwe Kumalo.

Although my colleagues in the English Department did not take part in the teaching of the course, they certainly played a role in influencing my ideas on African literature, particularly during our lively discussions on the literature syllabus of our Department. The presence of Ayi Kwei Armah in our midst was a blessing. Nobody could have been left unaffected by his dynamic approach to African literature. No man is an island. Our discussions in the English Department of the National University of Lesotho must have had a part to play in the formulation of my ideas. However, the theory of criticism and the analysis of novels presented here are my own, and nobody else should take any blame for the weaknesses of the book.

The theory of criticism presented in Part One of this book makes no claim to being more than an approach to African literature. The theory arose out of my concern with two problems, one universal and the other purely African.

The universal problem is the question of trying to bring together two closely related disciplines, linguistics and literary criticism. An attempt to bring these two disciplines together is in my opinion worthwhile and beneficial to both, particularly to literary criticism. These matters are discussed in greater detail in Chapter 2 of the first part of the book.

The second problem is the need to find an adequate method of studying the English of African writers. Early in 1977 I proposed to the English Department of the National University of Lesotho a course called 'the African Writer and the English Language' for senior students of African literature. Having obtained permission to teach the course, I was faced with the problem of how to present it. If the course was to be satisfactory, more than a mere repetition of what some critics have said about the use of English by African writers, I had to find a systematic method of teaching it, a sound theoretical basis from which to operate.

Details of the theoretical basis are discussed in Chapters 2 and 3. The approach presented operates on two basic principles: universality and particularity. Literature is a universal phenomenon. The three main genres — poetry, drama and fiction — are universal forms. Of course westerners will be quick to claim that the novel is a European form, that the realistic novel was first developed in the west. To this the African critic will answer: but the novel is a development of the tale, and the tale is a universal form. As far as written African literature is concerned, the tale goes as far back as the pyramid texts of ancient Egypt.[1] The Marxist critic may also add: form is socially conditioned. The novel is the result of historical conditions. It was occasioned by the rise of the bourgeoisie, and since bourgeois values first became prominent in Europe, it was natural that the novel should develop in Europe first.

Chinua Achebe has said that the African writer 'should aim at fashioning out an English which is at once universal and able to carry his peculiar experience'.[2] Maybe this is a good piece of advice for the critic of African literature. He should employ canons of criticism which are at once universal and capable of doing justice to the literature of his own particular nation. In other words, it is legitimate for the critic of African literature to focus on matters relevant to the African experience and African art, to focus on issues that confront African writers or which African writers have had to grapple with, at the same time without forgetting the universality of the nature and function of literature. It is my hope that the theory of criticism proposed in this volume can meet these two requirements.

Finally, let me explain the choice of the texts analysed in Part Two. There is one obvious and important omission — the works of Amos Tutuola. *The Palm-Wine Drinkard* should not be missed, if only because of its stylistic and historical significance, and was indeed included on our Lesotho course. For the purpose of this book, however, I decided to limit myself to writers and works which show a clear awareness of the social, political and ideological issues facing Africa today, to five novels that respond in one way or another to contemporary African problems. These five are of course not the only ones that show an awareness of the African condition, but they serve to demonstrate how stylistic criticism works and what it can reveal about African literature.

Another reason for the choice of these five texts is their artistic value. The five authors are among our most successful writers in Africa today, to all of whom English is a second language. A full discussion of their approaches to matters of style and technique should help our younger writers to be aware of the issues involved in the use of a foreign language in creative writing, and so to formulate their own ideas.

Notes

1 See Lichtheim, *Ancient Egyptian Literature*, pp. 21ff.
2 *Morning Yet on Creation Day*, p. 6.

Part One

The Theoretical Framework

1 Approaches to the Definition and Criticism of African Literature

▼▼▼▼▼▼▼▼▼▼▼▼▼▼▼▼▼▼▼▼▼▼▼▼▼▼▼▼▼

The debate on the criticism of African literature has focused on several related questions.

1. What is African literature?
2. Can western critics interpret African literature?
3. Is African literature part of the European tradition?
4. What is the correct approach to the criticism of African literature?

What follows is a brief account of some of the views which have been expressed on these questions.

In 1962 a conference of African writers in English failed to produce a satisfactory definition of 'African Literature'.[1] At another conference African literature was defined as 'creative writing in which an African setting is authentically handled or to which experiences originating in Africa are integral'.[2] According to this definition works produced by white writers like Nadine Gordimer, Doris Lessing and Alan Paton were included as part of African writing, while those by Conrad and Greene were excluded. A few years later Chinua Achebe attempted a definition: 'I do not see African literature as one unit but as a group of associated units — in fact the sum total of all *national* and ethnic literatures of Africa'.[3] By *national* literature Achebe refers to literature written in the national language of the nation, and by *ethnic* literature he means the literature written in one of the indigenous languages spoken by one group within the nation. More recently Nadine Gordimer, the white South African writer, has expressed views which incorporate those quoted here. For Gordimer, African writing is writing done 'in any language by Africans themselves and by others of whatever skin colour' who share the African experience and who have what she calls the 'Africa-centred consciousness'.[4]

The question whether western critics can play a role in the criticism of African literature has been the subject of much comment. At least two writers have expressed their views on the matter. In an essay entitled 'Colonialist Criticism' Achebe has castigated what he calls 'the colonialist critic'.[5] Achebe compares the attitude of the colonialist critic to that of the famous missionary, Albert Schweitzer, who declared that all men were brothers but the African was his younger brother. The colonialist critic is equally patronizing and arrogant, for he sees the

African writer 'as a somewhat unfinished European who with patient guidance will grow up one day and write like every other European'.[6] The colonialist critic shares one important feature with colonial administrators and officers: he claims supreme knowledge of the native. In the essay Achebe advises the European critic of African literature to cultivate humility and to get rid of his air of superiority and arrogance.

In another essay, 'Where Angels Fear to Tread', Achebe states: 'The question then is not whether we should be criticised or not, but what kind of criticism?'.[7] Here the Nigerian writer singles out three kinds of critics disliked by Africans: first, hostile critics; second, those critics who are amazed that Africans can write, and write in English too; third, those who say that African writers should be judged by the same standards as European writers, and then arrive at the logical conclusion that African writing is inferior to European writing. Achebe is at pains to point out that Europeans and Americans claim to know too much about Africa, when in actual fact they do not understand the African world view and cannot speak African languages.

Armah does not usually make public statements about his writing and about African literature in general, but he has made known his views on this discussion, in response to pronouncements made about him and his work by Charles Larson, author of *The Emergence of African Fiction*.

Armah's article is a strongly-worded attack on 'that style' of criticism 'which consists of the judicious distortion of African truths to fit western prejudices, the art of using fiction as criticism of fiction'.[8] On the question as to whether western critics can interpret African literature, Armah argues that the skilful interpreter operates within the framework of the prejudices of his readers, and so the western critic who 'does not operate from a plain and logical framework' but from 'a received framework of western values and prejudices' interprets literature for western readers whose interests are anti-African.[9] And he declares: 'western scholars, critics of African literature included, are nothing if not westerners working in the interests of the west'.[10]

Evidently, westerners themselves do not share these views. The large flow of critical comment that keeps on pouring out from the west is sufficient evidence that western critics do not believe themselves incapable of dealing with African literature. Some have in fact proposed critical procedures for African literature.[11]

The last two of our four questions are closely interrelated. If a critic regards African literature as part of European literature he will obviously use norms applied to European literature for evaluating African literature. The majority of western critics of African literature are probably of this view.

Among those who have made pronouncements on this matter may be included Edgar Wright (1973) who, without taking a very definitive position, sees African literature written in English as part of English literature. Wright does recognize some differences between English and

African literature, but for him African literature 'presents a particular problem within the broad field of literature in English'.[12]

Writing in *The Times Literary Supplement* from Rhodesia in 1973 T. O. McLoughlin addresses himself specifically to the novel genre and declares: 'The African novelists in English are not *sui generis*. They are writing within a generic and linguistic tradition which the reading public is conscious of.' He continues: 'The argument for critical separatism strikes one as unsound because it does not pay sufficient attention to this last point.'[13] McLoughlin's position is supported by M. R. Webb, who, writing from Nigeria, condemns the way literature is being taught in Africa now because, he says, literature is 'so bound up with politics, in a very simple way'.[14]

Some African critics have come very close to the positions of Wright and McLoughlin. Bahadur Tejani attacks what he calls 'dogmatists who insist on the singularity of literary tradition or effort' and 'circumscribe the writer to a particular philosophy or attitude'. Such critics, says Tejani, use only 'the subjective perception, which in many cases is simply what "Africa" means to him'. Tejani wants the critic to be free from 'isms' and 'tudes'.[15] Obiajunwa Wali, the controversial Nigerian critic, takes the linguistic criterion as the yardstick by which to measure whether African literature is African or European. The 'uncritical acceptance' of English and French as the medium of educated African writing is 'misdirected', says Wali, and 'has no chance of advancing African literature and culture'.[16] For African literature to be truly African it 'must be written in African languages'. Similarly, literary criticism of African writing sounds 'so dull, drab, flippant, mainly because there is no opportunity for original thinking'. Africans simply repeat European clichés like 'romantic', 'classic', 'realism', and so on. For Wali, therefore, African writing and criticism should be in African languages and critics should 'go in for the hard school of African linguistic studies' if they are to produce worthwhile criticism.

Another African critic, O. A. Ladimeji, is in complete disagreement with McLoughlin and Webb, and by implication, with Wali and Tejani. With reference to McLoughlin's letter referred to above, Ladimeji points out that McLoughlin 'identifies writing in English with belonging to the English literary tradition'. He closes the long debate in *The Times Literary Supplement* by declaring that 'African literature reverberates largely within the structures of African culture and history, on which English literature sheds very little light but much distortion'.[17] In an earlier letter Ladijemi tells us that his British students who were well read in English literature completely misunderstood African writers because they applied European norms of criticism to African writing, and he declares: 'The standards by which African literature is to be understood *issue* from that literature itself.'[18]

Chinua Achebe's views on the criticism of African writing by Africans may be summed up in one sentence: 'But there seems to me to be a genuine need for African writers to pause momentarily and consider whether anything in traditional African aesthetics will fit their contemporary condition.'[19] Some articles which have appeared in the journal *Okike*, of which Achebe is the editor, take up his suggestion by delving into the subject of African aesthetics. The article by Stanley Macebuh in *Okike* No. 5 is a good example.

My own opinion on all these issues is that the African critic cannot see himself in isolation from the African politician, philosopher, theologian, or educator, all of whom are looking for African solutions to their problems. The best of these and the truly African ones among them are striving to accelerate the processes of decolonization and liberation. In the same way, the African critic should search for African solutions in criticism, or should search for those solutions which, though not specifically African, will nevertheless do justice to African works of art. With regard to the second alternative, Marxist criticism seems to have much to offer to the critic of African literature.

But it is also my view that the African should be aware of the pitfalls of dogma. If we build a wall of dogma around us and refuse to see the rays of truth that may shine in Marxist criticism or in the west, we are surrendering ourselves to subjectivity and leading ourselves up a blind alley. The ultimate destination of a society which refuses to learn from other societies is parochialism and ignorant ethnocentrism!

In order to arrive at African standards of criticism we should accept whatever is good in Marxist criticism, whatever is useful in western criticism. But in order to liberate ourselves from foreign domination we should adopt our own viewpoint or viewpoints, as the case may be. Having a viewpoint does not necessarily mean abandoning ourselves to blind subjectivity. A viewpoint can lead to falsehood, self-deception and narrow mindedness if it is dogmatic; it can lead to freedom and truth if it is guided by honesty and objectivity. 'You can choose a viewpoint from which you will see nothing but fragments slipping into oblivion,' says Ernst Fischer, the Marxist critic, 'or one from which you can survey a wide range of reality in the process of creating new realities.'[20] One would like to think that those of us who believe in the search for African norms of criticism will choose the latter.

On the question of the definition of African literature, I am broadly in agreement with Achebe and Gordimer. However, among the majority of scholars of African literature there is very often an attempt to disregard literature written in the vernacular. True, the literature written in these languages is accessible only to a small portion of Africa, but it is nevertheless an expression of the African experience. Wali would of course go to the other extreme and say that 'any true African literature must be written in African languages', but that is not the view taken here. In spite of Wali's prophecy that African writers writing in English and French 'would be merely pursuing a dead end, which can only lead to sterility, uncreativity, and frustration',[21] we have seen the rise of a great literature during the last twenty years. Moreover, the signs are that, far from being frustrated, African writers writing in European languages are growing from strength to strength. This of course does not mean that Wali's contention is completely negative. Like Wali, I look forward to the development of African writing in African languages and, in particular, to the rise of an African language which can be used by all Africans as the African medium of artistic expression.

As regards the question of whether African literature is part of European literature, I prefer to tackle the problem from an African point of view. By this I mean that critics should sometimes stop to consider whether European literature is part of African literature. No doubt the overwhelming answer to this question is 'no'. It is inconceivable to think of European literature as part of African literature. But the reverse is often regarded as perfectly logical. For did Europe not father Africa? And do African writers not write in English, French and Portuguese? Do they not write in a linguistic tradition of which European readers are conscious? But arguments can be advanced to counter this kind of reasoning: when African nations become independent, does their literature remain part of European literature? Former colonies of Britain are no longer part of the British empire. And although African countries use English and French at OAU meetings, it would be absurd to argue that the OAU is a European organization.

But to say this is not to deny that Africa has been influenced by Europe. Colonialism and the slave trade have left an indelible mark on African history and culture, and many of our writers have responded vigorously to Europe's effect on Africa. And no doubt some African writers have been influenced directly by European literature. Thus Achebe's novel, *Things Fall Apart*, draws its title from Yeats' poem 'The Second Coming', and *No Longer at Ease* from T. S. Eliot's poem 'Journey of the Magi'. An understanding of these two poems will shed some light on the themes of the two novels. In Soyinka's poetry collection, *A Shuttle in the Crypt*, there are at least four poems whose titles are derived from archetypal figures found in European literature and the Bible: Joseph, Hamlet, Gulliver and Ulysses. Even some of the writers using indigenous African languages have been influenced by European literature. Thus Thomas Hardy's concept of destiny can be felt in T. K. Tsodzo's Shona novel, *Pafunge*.[22] To deny such facts would be as false as to deny that western European literature has been subject to external influences. The question to ask, however, is how much influence European literature has exerted on African literature, and to what extent can that influence be taken as the key to understanding and evaluating African literature.

African literature is part of world literature, just as Africa is part of humanity. Wellek and Warren did not have African literature in mind when they declared: 'Yet literature is one, as art and humanity are one.'[23] These two critics believe that individual nations make 'distinct contributions' to 'this general literary process'.[24] Likewise the relationship between African literature and world literature should be seen in the same light as that between African culture and world culture. African culture makes its own distinct contribution to world culture. Just because Africa was colonized and influenced by Europe, African culture should not be taken as part of European culture. There is a basic similarity underlying all literature of all nations, but cultural, historical, political and linguistic issues give rise to national differences. These are therefore factors which make African literature different from European, Latin American or Japanese literature. African literature springs from African social and historical conditions. It reflects problems — thematic, linguistic, aesthetic — which are peculiarly African.

What then makes Nigerian literature written in English closer to Kenyan literature than to British literature? First, the two nations share the common feature of Africanness. Second, they went through the same colonial experience. Third, and this is most important, there is no other continent in the world where different nations have the same sense of oneness as in Africa. Tribalism does exist, and certain forces, including some of our own politicians, are very busy trying to tear us apart, but the idea of one Africa is there in the minds of the people. This oneness is expressed in the aspirations of the OAU and in such songs as *Nkosi Sikelela i Africa/Ishe komborera Africa*, 'God Bless Africa', which many in southern Africa take as the national anthem of Africa. When I was young, I learned about the existence of the African nation before I knew that I belonged to a nation called 'Rhodesia'. Many of the songs we sang at school were about Africa and Africans, not about the Shona or Ndebele, the two major ethnic groups in the country. Despite the differences that distinguish one African nation from another, there is a common core of culture, political aspirations, history and world-view which binds the African people as one people. Many of our writers are conscious of these facts.

This discussion leads us to three conclusions. First, since literature is a universal phenomenon, there is a degree to which any competent reader of literature should be able to understand and interpret African literature, just as informed African readers should be in a position to pass judgement on non-African literature. Second, African literature issues from and reflects conditions which are peculiar to Africa. The critic should therefore endeavour to understand these conditions and should know Africa and her peoples well — if his pronouncements on African literature are to be genuine and free from European prejudices about Africa and African art. If a European critic knows Africa well, is honest and unbiased, and is a competent critic using sound critical standards relevant to African art, there is no reason why his pronouncements on African literature should not be as valid as those of informed African critics. Third, the search for norms of criticism which can do justice to African literature is necessary and worthwhile, but these norms should be based on aesthetic considerations, and not on purely political ones. In this connection it should be noted that European standards of criticism are themselves imperfect and are in need of further development.

Notes

1   See B. Modisane, 'African Writers' Summit', *Transition*, Vol. 2, No. 5.
2   See Ezekiel Mphahlele, 'African Literature and Universities', *Transition*, Vol. 4, No. 10.
3   Achebe, *Morning Yet on Creation Day*, p. 56.
4   *The Black Interpreters*, p. 5.
5   Achebe, 1975, op. cit., p. 3ff.
6   Ibid., p. 3.
7   Ibid., p. 46.
8   See 'Larsony or Fiction as Criticism of Fiction', *New Classic*, No. 4.
9   Ibid., p. 34.
10   Ibid., p. 44.
11   See, for instance, Wright, 1973.
12   Ibid., p. 21.
13   TLS, June 1, 1973, p. 617.
14   Ibid.
15   See Wanjala, *Standpoints on African Literature*, pp. 5–6.
16   Wali, 'The Dead End of African Literature?', *Transition*, Vol. 3, No. 10.
17   TLS, June 29, 1973, p. 749.
18   TLS, May 18, 1973.
19   See *Morning Yet on Creation Day*, p. 21.
20   *The Necessity of Art*, p. 110.
21   Wali, 1963, op. cit.
22   See T. K. Tsodzo (1972) *Pafunge*, Longman, Rhodesia.
23   *Theory of Literature*, p. 50.
24   Ibid., p. 52.

2 Linguistics, Literary Criticism and Stylistic Criticism

▼▼▼▼▼▼▼▼▼▼▼▼▼▼▼▼▼▼▼▼▼▼▼▼▼▼▼▼▼▼▼

What Contributions Can Linguistics Make to Criticism?

An African critic has said that language is 'the thing' by which we judge the success of the author.[1] Although a work of art consists of various elements — such as plot, theme, character and ideas — without language these elements would not be what they are; in other words they are realized and given form through the medium of language. In our analysis of literature, therefore, we need to have a sound understanding of the phenomenon called language, of its nature and functions.

Concerning the nature of language, we need not say more than that language is an exclusively human property consisting of a system of sounds, words, structures and meanings; that it is a symbolic system which does not necessarily show a one-to-one correspondence between itself and the physical world it refers to; that it is creative in the sense that the individual is capable of using it in a completely novel manner and can produce and understand sentences he has never heard before; and that it is a social convention which changes over time and is extremely adaptable to new conditions.

There are many different functions of language. They range from basic forms of communication, such as the cry of a hungry child, and more complex ones, such as political control, to self-expression: when a speaker or writer expresses himself in 'this form, these words and this order', simply to satisfy himself and to relieve himself of a burden of emotion within him. But the main function of language is to communicate, to give and receive messages. For any kind of verbal communication to take place, there must be a speaker and a hearer. The speaker speaks to be understood, to bring about a response from the hearer or audience. To get the correct response, the speaker must use language in a way that is understandable to the hearer. In other words, language is a common property shared by both the speaker and the hearer. If the speaker is to be understood, he cannot create his own private system of sounds, structures and meanings, but should operate within the confines of the communally owned communicative system —

a particular language in a particular community in a particular period of history.

The relationship between the writer and his audience, the reader, corresponds to that between the speaker and the hearer. A work of art is a communicative utterance from the speaker (writer) to the hearer (reader). It has a meaning which the writer conveys and to which the reader responds. It should be pointed out at the outset, however, that the 'meaning' of a work of art is different from purely informative utterances like: 'Mboya is coming here tonight', or 'Mugabe wants to see you'. The meaning of such utterances is cognitive and can be subjected to a purely rational analysis which involves no emotions. A work of art, on the other hand, contains the expressive and the affective. The writer expresses his own emotions, releases the tension in him, satisfies himself by expressing 'this thing in this form and these words', while at the same time he hopes to affect the reader, to evoke a certain kind of feeling in him or to persuade him either to take action or to see life in a new light. The meaning of a work of art is therefore not purely cognitive, it is emotive, it is affective; it is not subject to a purely rational analysis. A purely rational analysis of literature cannot do justice to literature, for literature is not scientific, and so a purely scientific approach to the study of literature can only kill the writer's creative effort.

However, literature is written in language, using the techniques and features of language, such as tone, grammatical structure, diction and metaphor. That is why, in order to arrive at a satisfactory understanding of literature, the reader must have an understanding of language, its function and its mode of operation. The reader must therefore have recourse to linguistics for a full understanding of the phenomenon of language. The study of linguistic structures, lexical meanings, sounds, rhythm, metre, language varieties, linguistic idiosyncracies — all these and much more are within the domain of the linguist. Thus the literary critic can only gain by making use of linguistic methods and the findings of linguistic research. The extent to which the critic can employ linguistic methods is a subject for further discussion; what should be emphasized here is that, if our understanding of literature is to some extent dependent on our understanding of the nature and functions of language, then progress in linguistic research must also mean progress in literary criticism.

The Goals of Stylistic Criticism

In this section I shall briefly explain the difference between stylistic criticism and related disciplines, starting with linguistics. The student of general linguistics is concerned with linguistic description, with the analysis of the various levels of language: the phonetic level, the grammatical, the lexical and the semantic level. The domain of the stylistician is narrower: he uses the principles of general linguistics to single out the distinctive features of a variety of the idiosyncracies of an author. He uses the principles of general linguistics to identify the features of language which are restricted to particular social contexts, and to account for the reasons why such features are used and when and where they are used.[2] The quantification of stylistic features to determine frequencies of occurrence is an important aspect of the stylistician's method. For his part the literary stylistician applies the methods of stylistics to the language of literature. The sociolinguist's domain is that of the relationship between language and society — the question of national languages, standard languages, dialects, orthographies, language contact, bilingualism, language and social class, and so on. But the distinction between the stylistician and the sociolinguist is not clear-cut, as the sociolinguist is very frequently called upon to use the methods of the stylistician — who is in turn called upon to make use of the techniques and principles of general linguistics. Thus general linguistics becomes the basis of other branches of linguistics which overlap with one another.

The stylistic critic *qua* stylistic critic cannot claim to take within his purview questions of national languages, languages of education, and so on, but he must be aware of them in so far as they are reflected in the work of art he is to analyse. He certainly must use the analytic tools of the linguist and stylistician; he must to some degree concern himself with minute details of grammar, lexis, phonology, prosody, meaning, as well as with the wider issues of deviation from the norm, the relationship between language and character, the relationship between the author and his audience. But more than that he must relate his analysis of linguistic features to considerations of content value and aesthetic quality in art. Lodge draws a distinction between the stylistician and the literary critic in the following manner: 'The stylistician seems obliged to rely upon an implied or accepted scale of values, or to put aside questions of value altogether; whereas the literary critic undertakes to combine analysis with evaluation.'[3] The stylistic critic, in our definition, is meant to bridge the gap between the stylistician and the critic as described by Lodge. He is as much interested in questions of value as the conventional critic, while at the same time he seeks to assimilate as much of the insights of stylistics as possible. Like the conventional critic he is interested in theme, plot and character, except that his interest is always related to the role that language plays in the delineation of these features of the novel.

The difference between stylistic criticism and conventional criticism is therefore one of both emphasis and method. It may be summarized as follows.

1. Stylistic criticism seeks to bring the methods and insights of linguistics into literary criticism.
2. It aims at being more precise and more systematic than conventional criticism.
3. It places much greater emphasis on the language component of

literature than does conventional criticism.

4. But unlike stylistic analysis proper and unlike literary stylistics, it endeavours to avoid a purely technical approach to the study of literature and is as much concerned about matters of aesthetic value and content as conventional criticism.

Notes

1 B. I. Chukwukere, 'The Problem of Language in African Creative Writing', *African Literature Today*, No. 3.
2 See, for instance, Crystal and Davy, *Investigating English Style*, p. 10.
3 *Language of Fiction*, p. 56.

3 Towards a Theory of Stylistic Criticism

▼▼▼▼▼▼▼▼▼▼▼▼▼▼▼▼▼▼▼▼▼▼▼▼▼▼▼▼▼▼▼▼▼

At its most general level, the theory of stylistic criticism proposed here is intended to embrace all art-forms, that is poems, novels and plays. But in this book it is applied specifically to works of fiction, and so we shall concern ourselves with this particular genre. The starting point of our analysis is an acceptance of the fact that a work of art, like other language acts, is a communicative utterance produced by the author and received by the reader. The link between the author and the reader is the art-form itself, as shown below:

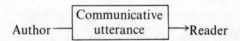

The reader's response will depend on three major variables: the nature of the utterance, what the author says and how he says it; the reader's own competence and experience in appreciating literary works of art; and the usefulness of the method and approach adopted by the reader.

A competent and experience reader will respond more adequately to a work of art than someone who is less competent. As our concern here is with works of art and tools of analysis, we shall pay greater attention to the first and last of these variables. For a theory of literary criticism to be an adequate theory, it should give an account of the nature of works of art and should provide the student of literature with a framework of analysis and method of evaluation. I would agree with Crane that 'the final test of any critical language is what its particular scheme of concepts permits or encourages us to say, in practical criticism, about individual works'.[1]

The theory of stylistic criticism proposed here is three-dimensional.
1. It gives an account of the constituents of a work of art and an account of the dimensions of the language of fiction.
2. It lays down a set of criteria for evaluating fiction from the point of view of stylistic criticism.
3. It has a basic critical terminology.

At the level of constituent elements, the theory gives an analysis of the various components of the communicative utterance which combine to produce the meaning and aesthetic effect of a work of art. At the level of evaluation, we set out what is to be evaluated and how the evaluation is to be done. There is not enough room for a complete account of all the terms used in criticism, but the key terms in the critical terminology are defined and classified.

The Constituents of Fiction and the Determinants of Linguistic Format

The account of the constituents of fiction presented here differs in some respects from traditionally accepted ideas about the structure of the novel. Since the publication of E. M. Forster's *Aspects of the Novel* in 1927, many works have been published on the subject. The reader may refer to the following, among others: Hardy,[2] Bradbury,[3] Boulton[4] and the collection of essays edited by Robert Murray Davis.[5] In the Marxist tradition, Georg Lukács has produced valuable work, including his two well-known books, *Studies in European Realism* (1972) and *The Historical Novel* (1962).

In my view, fiction can be analysed into four main constituents: content, narrative structure, character and linguistic format. The novelist sets out to talk about something: it may be love, liberation, culture, religion, or an imaginative idea. What he sets out to write about is the subject-matter. He is saying something about the subject-matter; he is expressing his views about people, society and life in general. He is telling us what his attitude is to the subject-matter and, in the process, influences our own views on the questions he raises; or at least makes us think about them. What he says about the subject-matter is the theme of the novel. In a novel there may be several themes, one being dominant and the others subsidiary. The subject-matter, the theme, the views and attitudes expressed by the writer, as well as the meaning of the artefact, or what we may call its 'message' — all of these constitute the content. In a realistic novel the content is socially conditioned, it issues from historical conditions, it is a record of the author's response to his social environment.

The backbone of a work of fiction is what is usually called the plot. The plot holds the various elements of the novel together and gives it a structure. It is a story, a sequence of events arranged in a time-chain from the beginning to the end. The events have a causal relationship with one another; in other words, one event leads into and determines another. But the author will not necessarily narrate the events chronologically. He may start with the beginning or with the middle or with the end of the story and avoid a purely sequential structure. He may present his story in the form of flashbacks, turning the reader's mind to the present, to the future and to the past — again avoiding a purely sequential structure. In telling the story, the author also adopts what is called a point of view. In other words the author can present his story through the eyes of an individual character, who tells the story in the form of *I*, the first person. Everything that happens is seen from this narrator's point of view. The author theoretically stands outside the story. A writer can also assume the omniscient narrator point of view and describe the events as if he knows what goes on in the minds of all his characters, or of some of them. Usually the main character receives the greatest attention from the author. Here the story is told in the third person, in the form of *he*. There are other variations and combinations of points of view but one thing is clear: whatever point of view he adopts, the author is behind the story he tells. He is behind the *I*, the *he*, the *we* or whatever he uses. Now this arrangement of the episodes which make up the story, this ordering of incidents in a pattern, together with the point of view adopted by the author, is what we call the narrative structure. The term 'narrative structure' is therefore broader in meaning than 'plot', because the latter excludes the point of view.

In order to tell a story, the novelist must have characters; the actors in the drama of the novel, the people who populate the world of the novel. In this volume characters are also referred to as 'participants' in accordance with linguistic practice. By participants we mean those imaginative creations of the author who interact with each other, who participate in the action of the novel and who are used as the author's agents in his communicative utterance.

The story of the novel is told in words, in the medium of language. The writer selects lexical items, grammatical structures and symbols, to talk about his subject, to create characters, to bring out his theme. In other words he uses a linguistic format. The linguistic format is the realization of content, character and narrative structure into a verbal object, what we call the novel. Content, character and narrative structure do not exist outside the verbal structure. The meaning of an utterance is the result of the combination of particular words in a particular sequence. Thus the following strings of words mean different things:

> 'You are kind.'
> 'You are here.'
> 'Are you here?'

The second differs from the first because of the choice of words. In the second 'kind' is replaced by 'here' and this results in a very different meaning. In terms of choice of words the second and the third are exactly the same, but the organization, the sequence, is different and this, again, results in different meanings. In the same way the content of a work of fiction is definable in terms of the writer's choice of words and in his organization of the entire verbal structure. The picture we get of a character is the result of what the author says about him, what he, the character, says and does, and what other characters say about him. The narrative structure is indeed the result of a sequence of incidents and events, but these are realized through the medium of language. The narrative structure, characterization and the linguistic format constitute what is normally called 'form' in criticism.

The linguistic format is the sum total of minute linguistic choices, which are divisible into two sub-sets: linguistic features proper, and para-linguistic affective devices. By 'para-linguistic affective devices' we mean such features as symbolism, myth, allusion, allegory, which are not analysable in terms of normal linguistic description. Under 'linguistic features proper' we isolate several levels of description as follows.

1. The grammatical level, where we consider questions of syntax, sentence type and the relationship between meaning and form.
2. The phonological level, which includes rhyme, rhythm, alliteration, assonance etc.
3. The lexical level, where we consider the writer's choice of words, the collocations of words, metaphors, similes, their effects and their meanings.
4. The level of tenor of discourse which comprises tone and the degree of formality and informality between the participants in the drama of the novel and between the author and the reader.
5. The graphological level at which we consider how the print, the colour and shape of the printed marks, punctuation and paragraphing contribute to the aesthetic appeal and readability of a work of art.

These visual features can be exploited by the writer to evoke certain kinds of feeling in the reader. An example which is often cited is George Herbert's poem, 'Easter Wings', which is constructed in the form of wings and whose appeal is partly determined by the appearance of the printed marks on the page.

The writer's choice of individual linguistic features and ultimately of the entire linguistic format, together with the reader's response to the linguistic format and the aesthetic quality of a work of art, are determined by a number of interacting factors which may be termed the 'determinants' of the linguistic format. These are:

Medium
Mode
Language/dialect
Context
Field of discourse
Participants/participating agents
Audience
Personal factors

Let us now define the eight determinants.

Medium

The medium is the method used to communicate language. Linguists have drawn a distinction between *written* language and *spoken* language, the difference being that the one is transmitted in the form of printed marks and the other through air as sound. A spoken utterance is received through the ear and a written one through the eye. A novel is read, it is not heard. Another distinction that should be made is that between what I call the *audio-phonic* medium (the radio) and the *visual audio-phonic* medium (television). Each medium has its own characteristics and may require a method of analysis which is peculiar to its nature.

A medium can be *authentic* or *simulated*. For example, conversations in novels are meant to represent spoken language, and so when we examine a dialogue in a novel as a piece of language, we are dealing with a simulated medium.

Mode

Works of art can be classified according to mode and modal characteristics. Mode as defined here refers to what is normally called 'form'. The term 'mode' is more satisfactory than 'form' because the latter has a more general application, referring to both the external and the internal structure, for instance, cohesiveness and patterning, and is often loosely used; whereas we can restrict the meaning of 'mode' to what we may call the 'genre' of the work under discussion. The distinction between one mode and another operates at different levels, from the most general to the most specific. The primary distinction that I want to make is between the genres or 'kinds' of literature, that is prose, fiction, poetry and drama. Within these genres, a secondary distinction can be made between the various modes. Thus prose fiction can be classified into fantasy fiction — the romance and folk tales — and realistic fiction — the novel and the short story. Poems can be subcategorized into, for instance, epic poems, lyrics, ballads, sonnets, praise poems. Plays are classified into tragedies, comedies, histories. Each of these modes will to some extent determine the linguistic content of a work of art. In the realistic novel, the element of characterization, which is an intrinsic feature of the mode, gives rise to different linguistic choices depending on the cultural and linguistic background of various characters and on their relationship with one another.

Language/dialect

This determinant represents the writer's broadest linguistic choice. It may be called the 'macrocosmic' level of the writer's linguistic choice, where he is concerned with the question of which language and which dialect to use. For most mother tongue speakers, the question does not arise at its most general level. It is taken for granted that writers like Graham Greene, Ernest Hemingway or T. S. Eliot write in English. It may be important to them which dialect of English they use. For the African writer, however, the question often arises at its most general level. Is he to write in English or in his mother tongue? If in English, in which variety or dialect? Thus a writer may choose to use Standard English, which falls into two main international branches, British English and American English. He may choose to use a dialect that has developed in his own country — we shall call it a local African standard. He may use a sub-standard dialect such as West African pidgin. He may find it necessary to make use of a transliterated form, expressing himself in English words, but in a manner consonant with the idioms and structures of his mother tongue. Finally, he may decide to combine any of these varieties depending on his aesthetic purpose and on the participants in the novel.

Context

The cultural context, the geographical setting and the historical period during which a work of art is written will in part determine the linguistic choices open to the writer. A writer can of course reach a very high degree of distinctiveness and can excel in making use of linguistic devices and modes of expression that are peculiarly his own. But however idiosyncratic he may be, he cannot avoid the imprint of history and culture. Shakespeare was a great writer, but his language belongs to the Elizabethan period just as Chaucer's English can only be fully understood and appreciated by placing it in the context of Middle English. Thus one condition for understanding literature is that of placing it in its cultural, geographical, historical and ideological context. It has been said that 'all linguistic performance makes reference to recognized cultural conventions of a regular and restrictive kind' and that one can actually draw a diagram of a community's structure by 'making a classification of its modes and styles of linguistic performance'.[6] A language is not only words and grammatical structures: the use of a language carries with it prejudices, habits and mannerisms of its native speakers.

All these facts are of great importance and relevance to our evaluation of African literature written in English. The African writer's position is a complex one. His chosen tongue is not his own, neither is it his own people's language. His society has its own linguistic system with its own prejudices and world views, while his chosen language reflects those of its native speakers. Furthermore he is himself caught between two or three conflicting cultures. Ethnically bound to his own people, he is by his education western-oriented, while he is sometimes in sympathy with eastern ideology. His culture is of a very complex nature. It is no longer simply African, but has been penetrated by influences from the west, while the socialist ideology of Russia and China receives a sympathetic hearing from many progressive African thinkers. All these factors have a bearing on the writer's technique and linguistic choices.

The importance of context to literary composition and criticism has been emphasized by Ernst Fischer, the Marxist critic. To him the social context in which a work of art is written, what he calls 'the social element', is crucial: 'An analysis of style, however intelligent it may be and however brilliant its insight into specific problems and details, is bound to fail unless it recognizes that content — that is to say, in the last instance, the social element — is the decisive style-forming factor in art.' So to do justice to any work of literature, we must study 'the social conditions, movements and conflicts of the period, the class relationships and struggles and the resulting ideas'.[7]

Field of discourse

In stylistic analysis the linguistic elements discussed under 'field of discourse' are those features which are seen to characterize a particular area of language activity, such as a profession or a specific occupational activity. Thus law, advertising and religious worship are regarded as constituting different fields of discourse, each with its own distinguishing linguistic features. Field of discourse is probably the least important determinant of linguistic choice in a novel and is very difficult to define in the context of literature. In discussing this determinant we should take into account the subject of the work of fiction under discussion, as the subject is likely to influence, in some measure at least, the writer's choice of lexical items. Thus in Achebe's *A Man of the People*, a book about politics, we meet a considerable number of political catchwords, slogans and economic terms; while in George Orwell's *Animal Farm*, a novel about a socialist revolution, we find many words referring to socialist ideas. While this is true in a very broad sense, the stylistic critic should take stock of the fact that a work of art is much more complex than a piece of scientific or religious writing. Granted that the subject of the book as a whole is likely to influence the writer's linguistic choices, it is important to remember that different parts of the book, the individual episodes, may be about different fields of discourse which cut across each other, so that the interaction of all these 'local' fields of discourse results in a very complex mixture of language varieties. Thus field of discourse in a work of fiction can be seen to operate at two levels, the general and the specific or local. A further complication in the definition of this determinant is that a creative writer is not limited by considerations of language registers. He may talk of one thing in terms of another and thus make use of a completely different field of discourse from that which his subject matter naturally falls under. *Animal Farm* is about human beings, but Orwell discusses the predicament of man in terms of an animal allegory so that the novel is characterized by lexical items referring to animals.

Participants/participating agents

At this level we identify the participants whom the primary utterer, the author, has used as his agents in the language act. There are two main types of participants, the narrator and the interlocutors or characters. The narrator tells the story and describes events, characters and objects.

The interlocutors are involved in conversation, discussion or internal monologue. The two types of agents we have described can be said to give rise to three modes of language in the novel: narrative, description, dialogue and internal monologue. As the participants are not all of equal status we take into consideration the status, background and role of each participant in the drama of the novel. An interlocutor may be a young person or an elder in an African society; he may be educated or uneducated; he may be a mother tongue speaker of the language or a second language speaker. His background and status will often determine the type of language that a participant uses. In real life no two individuals speak a language in exactly the same way. The speech characteristics, the language of a particular individual or interlocutor are called his 'idiolect'. In the same way a character in a novel may have idiosyncrasies which constitute his idiolect.

Audience

The relationship between the writer and his audience is important in a number of respects. A writer writing for children should be conscious of the level of sophistication and linguistic attainment that is expected of that kind of audience. An African writing about Africa with an African audience in mind will have a different orientation from a European writing about Africa with a European audience in view. Two critics of African literature may be cited as examples. Charles Larson in *The Emergence of African Fiction*, and Harold Collins in *Amos Tutuola*, are writing about Africa but with a western audience in view and so there is much in what they say which is revolting to an African readership.[8] Indeed an African writer writing about Africa with a European audience in mind is likely to adopt a different attitude and a different style from an African writing about Africa with an African audience in view. Very often the African writer has both audiences in view so that the distinction between the one and the other may not come out in clear-cut terms. We are also concerned with a narrower dimension of the author–reader relationship — the tenor of discourse. According to Spencer and Gregory, tenor of discourse is concerned with 'the degree of formality in the situation which the language mirrors, which can be said generally to depend upon the relationship between the speaker (or writer) and hearer (or reader)'.[9] Though accepting this definition, we shall widen the concept slightly to include the attitude of the author to his audience and, where this is applicable, to the object of his criticism or to the subject generally. In spoken language a speaker may be polite, impolite, or reserved in relation to his audience and to the object of criticism — the latter applies to cases where the speaker is criticising something or somebody. His attitude to his audience and to the object of his criticism will be reflected in his tone of voice as well as his choice of words. Thus he may choose a tone of voice and words which show respect to his audience and to the subject or object of criticism, or he may employ a tone of voice and a set of words which are disparaging either to the victim or to both victim and audience. Sometimes he can offend the audience not by a deliberate choice of words and tone, but simply by failing to define his intended relationship with his audience. One day a young Mosotho man who had just finished his studies in America was invited to give a talk at a seminar in Lesotho. He spoke with an American accent using many Americanisms. As a result of this some members of the audience staged a walk-out. They were annoyed by the speaker's tenor of discourse. In other words we may call tenor of discourse 'the tone of the telling'.[10]

Personal factors

Here we consider the writer's competence in using the chosen language, his own personal interests, his experience, natural inclinations, as well as his views and turn of mind. These things have some influence on what he is going to write about and on the attitude and tone of voice he is going to adopt, and ultimately on the linguistic content of his artistic creation. T. S. Eliot's themes and technique, for example, are closely connected with his own beliefs and intellectual concerns. The same applies to Yeats. The references to gyres, to Egyptian civilization and to Byzantium all reflect his philosophy and interests. To have a full understanding of a writer, therefore, often requires a knowledge of these personal factors.

Evaluation Criteria

We evaluate a work of art in terms of the following criteria:
1. Readability — the writer's ability to communicate with the reader, the rate at which the competent reader can go through the book, and the relative ease or difficulty with which he does so.
2. The appropriateness and effectiveness of the writer's choice of linguistic features and para-linguistic affective devices considered in relation to the eight determinants of the linguistic format.
3. The content value and aesthetic quality of the artistic creation as a whole, content and aesthetic quality being seen in dialectical interaction with one another.

Readability

Readability is the result of a number of interacting factors. The style of the writer has an important part to play. A simple style is often easy to cope with, while the use of involved sentences and unusual words may result in difficulties for the reader. But an easy style is not necessarily a good indication of a novel's readability, neither does a complex style necessarily hinder readability. A dull book written in a simple style can bore the reader stiff and tempt him to throw it away. Joseph Conrad's language in *Heart of Darkness* is far from simple and yet the story has a power that compels the reader to go on reading it. T. S. Eliot's poetry is extremely difficult to understand, but the poet's language has such a magic grip on the reader that in spite of inability to comprehend the 'literal meaning' he is persuaded to go on reading in order to experience the 'aesthetic meaning' of the poetry. The aesthetic appeal of the writer's language is thus one aspect of a novel's readability.

The aesthetic appeal may be regarded as determining the writer's power of persuasion. A writer, like a preacher or politician, has to keep his audience interested, and one way in which he does so is by using rhetoric.

Readability is also determined by the writer's handling of character and plot, for these have a force that sustains the reader's interest. A plot that is well handled helps the reader to follow the story and thus to keep his interest, while his identification with characters along with the writer's other techniques, such as suspense, will help to increase his curiosity and his desire to go on reading. The handling of language, plot and character may be so powerful that the reader is gripped by a magnetic force which compels him to plough through the book with gusto until the very end. A novel which attracts the reader in this way is, in our scheme, not only persuasive, but also compelling. Readability can be measured in terms of low, average or high. A book that is not readable or that has a low readability, a work that is not persuasive and not compelling, may be described as 'inhibiting' because it inhibits the reader and forces him to put it away unfinished.

The appropriateness and effectiveness of linguistic choices and para-linguistic affective devices

The writer's use of language may be judged in relation to the same eight determinants of linguistic format.

MEDIUM   At the level of medium we expect the creative artist to be aware of the nature of his chosen medium and of the limitations it imposes upon him. Written language, for example, is often required to be more explicit than spoken language because the meaning conveyed by the latter depends to a very large extent on the context of situation which is of course denied to written language. In a real conversation an interlocutor can suddenly say 'That is very beautiful' without specifying in words what the beautiful thing is. He can do this without running the risk of being misunderstood because he is able to point at the object he has referred to as being beautiful. In a novel the object is not there for us to see, and so the writer has to give more information about it in order to help his readers to understand. In English, stress and intonation are denied to writing; naunces of meaning brought about by exploiting these features in spoken language will be lost unless the writer makes use of accepted conventions where they exist. Italicising will often show the reader where a word is stressed, and the question mark distinguishes a question from a statement expressed in the same string of words.

MODE   The writer should handle the various elements of the language of fiction well — narrative, description, dialogue and monologue. It has to be remembered that unlike the lyric poem, the novel is a long form demanding a lot of the reader's time and attention. It can therefore be argued that a novel cannot be expected to be as dense and concentrated as a lyric poem. Poetic prose is indeed a virtue and a talented writer can lend a poetic quality to his prose. But people do not normally speak in poetry, and so dialogue in a novel should approximate to the language of everyday life, which is characteristically prosaic.

LANGUAGE/DIALECT   Language is a very important component of the verbal arts. To be able to write effectively and artistically, the writer himself must have achieved a high degree of competence in his chosen language. This competence can only be demonstrated by his ability to mould the chosen dialect into a fit medium of artistic creation. Whether the writer chooses his own language or Standard English or another dialect of English, the first requirement is that he should be at home with the language so that whatever linguistic devices he employs in his work, whether simple deviations from the norm or translations from another language, are in the final analysis products of a genuine artistic concern, not a reflection of the author's inability to handle the language effectively. Lack of proficiency in the chosen language limits the choices open to the writer and can often lead to artificiality, monotony and mediocrity.

CONTEXT   It has been said above that a diagram of a community's structure may be drawn by 'making a classification of its modes and styles of linguistic performance'. This seems to present a difficulty for writers using a foreign language as the instrument of their artistic expression. If language is an expression of culture, and if the map of a culture is isomorphic with the network of its communicative systems, how does the African writer using English channel his artistic expression? Is not one of his preoccupations to present a critique of colonialism along with its modes of thinking, which are reflected in the colonial language? Does he simply map out English culture for an African audience or, for that matter, for a western audience expecting to be told about African culture, African views and African ways of comprehending reality? In *The Forsaken Lover* Chris Searle has shown how language is used as a weapon of colonization, subordination and cultural deprivation; how for centuries the black man has spoken a version of the white man's language 'in which the qualities of whiteness meant purity and goodness and the qualities of blackness degradation and devilishness'.[11] In view of this, what system of symbols and myths does the African writer of English expression use? The success of the African writer here will depend on his sensitiveness to all these issues and on his ability to mould the foreign language into a fit medium for the expression of national culture, national aspirations, the African temperament and the expression of the human predicament as seen through African eyes.

FIELD OF DISCOURSE   We have already seen how the field of discourse is not easy to define in a work of fiction, how different registers of language can cut across each other, and how the creative writer can describe one thing in terms of another. But whatever the technique of the writer, whatever his method of handling language registers, the stylistic critic must judge the appropriateness and effectiveness of the author's linguistic choices. He will demand, for instance, that a conversation be natural and lifelike, unless there are artistic and convincing reasons for its being unnatural and unrealistic.

PARTICIPANTS   The relationship between language and participants is important in terms of verisimilitude and decorum. We expect the writer to take stock of the social status and linguistic background of his characters. The novel is a realistic species of literature, a realistic mode. In real life, we do not normally expect an uneducated village man to speak in a European language except where it is clear that the language in which the character originally spoke is assumed to have been his native tongue. We do not expect the majority of African speakers of English to use an Oxford or New York accent. Conversely we would be surprised to hear all of Achebe's characters speaking pidgin, if pidgin is the language associated with the urbanized African, not those who live in the village and have their roots in the village. Should an elder in Umuaro, a group of villages in Eastern Nigeria (see *Arrow of God*), address his fellow elders in pidgin English or in the English of the parent country, England? The author may attribute a native-like variety of English to the interlocutors in a dialogue, but what effect does this have on the reader? Does the use of such a dialect not have an adverse effect on verisimilitude? What of the author who takes upon himself the role of narrator: what dialect should he use?

Achebe has pointed out the importance of writing in character, the importance of relating language to character and of judging what is or is not appropriate. Illustrating his own approach to the problems of writing in English, he takes an extract from *Arrow of God* and shows how he handles the language of Ezeulu, the Chief Priest. Ezeulu uses idioms that are consonant with the modes of expression of the Igbo people. By way of contrast, Achebe then translates Ezeulu's words into conventional English and remarks: 'The material is the same. But the form of the one is *in character* and the other is not.'[12] And talking about tragedy, Aristotle has emphasized the relationship between the choice of language and the delineation of character: 'Character is that which reveals personal choice, the kinds of thing a man chooses or rejects when that is not obvious. Thus there is no revelation of character in speeches in which the speaker shows no preferences or aversions whatever'.[13]

AUDIENCE   The importance of the author–reader relationship has already been emphasized in the previous section. This relationship may be defined by the tenor of discourse. Spencer and Gregory have said: 'a poet or a novelist having chosen to use a particular tenor, for the purpose of defining his intended relationship with his reader, certain linguistic consequences will follow...'[14] A creative writer may argue that as an artist he should not be limited by the norms of linguistic behaviour in his society, since style can in fact be described as 'deviation from the norm'. However, decorum is important, even for the creative writer. The tastes of the reading public cannot be completely ignored without the author running a risk. It is possible for a writer to offend his readers by deliberately using language in a manner that is seen to breach linguistic decorum. Politeness and privacy belongs as much to language as they do to social relationships. Matters of etiquette extend beyond actions to verbal expressions, and the writer is called upon to be sensitive to the tastes of his readers in the sphere of verbal etiquette. It could be argued that some African writers have become unusually blunt and unreserved in matters relating to sex and human excrement. Unless such bluntness is justifiable in terms of aesthetic purpose, as in Armah's *The Beautyful Ones Are Not Yet Born*, then it is certain to offend, shock or alienate part of the writer's audience. True, the artist may wish to train his readers to rise above the superstitious fear of taboos and emotive words, he may be motivated by a desire to teach his readers to take a technological view of language — that language is simple a tool to be used in any way the user wants — but he cannot avoid the cold reality that emotions are as much part of language as they are part of human life. A writer may find using language in an unconventional manner a very stimulating experience. Sometimes, far from alienating the reader, the writer's ability to shock may be the very source of his work's popularity, as is the case with Maillu's *After 4.30*. But the yardstick for measuring artistic value is not popularity, it is aesthetic quality and moral earnestness.

PERSONAL FACTORS   To nave a full understanding of an author it is sometimes necessary to know more than the cultural and historical context in which he writes; very often it is also important to be familiar with his own interests, his views of the world and his attitude to art. Here the reader should try to meet the artist on his own terms.

That said, it should also be pointed out that on one level art is a combination of two forces in dialectical interaction — the expressive and the communicative. The writer sets out to express himself, to satisfy the creative urge in him. He wants to express his own feelings, his own emotions, or to express an idea or describe life in a manner most satisfying to himself. But at the other end is the reading public. Of course, the writer cannot be guided by the dictates of the reading public, for that way lies the destruction of his creative genius. But the artist cannot afford to ignore the public completely, he cannot be a slave to the creative urge at the expense of the communicative purpose. A writer who becomes entirely egocentric, satisfied with a purely personal system of symbols, images and thought runs the risk of being misunderstood. T. S. Eliot's early poetry contains symbols which are difficult to decipher, but even there Eliot found salvation in 'the objective correlative', a mode of expression which enabled him to evoke the emotions he wanted to excite in the reader.[15]

The writer can be ingenious, can demonstrate linguistic dexterity of the highest order, but if his mastery of language is not controlled by the aesthetic purpose it can become a means of self-gratification and self-glorification, and can thus defeat the communicative purpose of art. The artist may of course argue that he is not concerned with communication, but we are bound to agree with Richards when he says: 'the reluctance of the artist to consider communication as one of his main aims, and his denial that he is at all influenced in his work by a desire to affect other people, is no evidence that communication is not actually his principal object'.[16]

If obscurity is a danger, so also is uncontrolled emotion. The pouring out of emotions can defeat art by becoming another form of self-gratification, a form of indulgence in feelings and emotions, or in the expression of them. Ernst Fischer has said that the artist's work is not a state of 'intoxicated isnpiration'. The artist must learn how to transform experience and emotion into form. 'The passion that consumes the dilettante *serves* the true artist: the artist is not mauled by the beast, he tames it.'[17] Eliot has expressed the same idea in terms of the writer's striving towards impersonality: 'Poetry is not a turning loose of emotion, but an escape from emotion; it is not the expression of personality, but an escape from personality.'[18] 'The progress of an artist', Eliot says, 'is a continual self-sacrifice, a continual extinction of personality.' The artist must surrender himself to 'something which is more valuable'.[19] This matter of emotion and self-sacrifice cannot be completely divorced from the question of the relationship between the author and the audience discussed above. The writer who seeks to express certain kinds of emotion in a manner pleasing to himself but disturbing to the reader, without convincing reasons, can be said to be subjecting the artistic purpose to his personality instead of depersonalizing himself for the sake of art.

Content value and aesthetic quality

Just as language has a social function in human society so too does literature. In traditional African communities the literary modes of song, folktale and praise poem had a social function. Among the Shona people, as among other African peoples, each human activity was associated with its own type of song. There were war songs, thrashing songs, marriage songs, drinking songs, funeral songs — songs for all social occasions. Traditional stories had an important moral lesson behind them. Some taught the customs and traditions of the community; some trained young men and women to endure hardships; some taught young men to be brave and fearless warriors; some were social satires. There were indeed some stories whose main function was to entertain and not to teach, but the more serious ones had an important message. There was much excitement and much enjoyment in these stories, but there were also serious things to learn from them. The bard was an entertainer and a teacher.

In the modern world the role of the ancient bard has been delegated to the creative writer. If we no longer sit by the fireplace listening spellbound to the enchanting narrative and song of the grey-haired grandmother, we now spend our evenings reading Achebe's novels to each other, or silently to ourselves. Just as the ancient bard had a social function, had a lesson to teach, so the modern writer too has a social function, has something to say to us. A serious writer must be concerned about humanity and his society; a serious African writer must address himself to the human predicament in general and to the African situation in particular. In short we expect moral earnestness from the writer, we expect to be informed about man and life just as we expected to acquire wisdom from the storyteller's tale. Indeed entertainments have their place in society — true art should not be confounded with political and ideological propaganda — but art for art's sake cannot be justified in a world struggling against disease, illiteracy, racialism, oppression, imperialism and exploitation.

But just as the ancient bard did not teach us by boring us, just as his moral was not imposed upon us but was something we looked forward to, the writer must not force his moral down our throats by boring us. The writer is a healer of our minds and souls. If he wants to heal our ills he should not give us sour pills; we shall merely taste them and then spit them out. To be a successful healer, the writer should bring us a pill concealed in a lump of sugar. It is then that we will taste, suck and swallow the pill and be healed. The message or meaning of a work of art should be like a parcel that is beautifully wrapped. Our job as stylistic critics is to judge the success of the writer's wrapping technique in relation to the value of the article in the parcel. The wrapping technique and the value of the article are of equal importance.

The analogies I have drawn above and my analysis of the constituent parts of a work of fiction give rise to the question: is there a clear-cut dichotomy between linguistic format and content, or to phrase the question in more conventional terms, between form and content? It is a tendency of the human mind to abstract just as it is a function of language to classify features of the physical world into separate entities. Thus a tree is divided into roots, stem and branches, and man talks about his body, his mind, his soul, his hair and his ego. We abstract in order to comprehend the object of discussion more fully, in order to be able to talk about it. It is therefore convenient and useful to talk about content and form in art; it is also convenient and useful, albeit justifiable, to talk about content, character, narrative structure and linguistic format. In fact the content is only definable in terms of the artistic creation as a whole, in terms of the total aesthetic effect of the work of art, an effect that is the result of a dynamic and complex interaction of events, people, ideas, attitudes and words. A perfect work of art is a synthesis of reality, subject matter, theme, views, attitudes and ideas on the one hand, and narrative structure, character and linguistic format on the other. What the artist intended to say prior to composition is not necessarily what the finished work says. What the finished work says and means to the reader depends on how the author says it. Fischer has emphasized the unity of content and form by saying: 'content is not only *what* is presented but also *how* it is presented'.[20] That the content and the linguistic components of an artistic creation cannot be separated can be proved by the simple fact that a poem or novel cannot be paraphrased. To read a paraphrase of a poem or novel is to read another poem or novel — in fact a paraphrase can completely kill a work of art. No one who has not read a book can claim to know the book, for knowledge of a work of art means experiencing it, and we can only experience it by reading through it, by reacting to the writer's handling of plot, theme and character through the medium of language. The value of the article in the parcel is only definable in terms of the wrapping technique.

Marxist criticism maintains that form is socially conditioned.[21] Form is the result of historical, social and ideological factors. The novel for instance resulted from a change in ideological orientation. It was the result of the rise of the bourgeois class which challenged the older aristocratic order and held individual material achievements supreme. In other words the novel developed simultaneously with the rise of capitalism and western individualism. Similarly it can be said that the various modes of poetry and song we have cited as having existed in traditional African society were socially conditioned. The various literary modes were the direct result of different categories of human activity so that these forms were determined by the content — by the activity and the social context.

The argument advanced above serves to clarify a very important aspect of stylistic criticism. The theory of stylistic criticism proposed here holds that matters of linguistic format are inseparable from the content. In other words, the style of a serious writer cannot be divorced from his ideological concerns. To extract passages from a purely linguistic point of view without any regard to theme and subject-matter is like treating a patient without diagnosing the disease — the chances are that the disease will not be cured. Similarly stylistic analysis *per se* or what Chapman calls 'literary stylistics' is inadequate. It treats style apart from theme and subject-matter and thus seeks to separate form and content in works of art.

The Classification of Critical Terminology

It is the aim of stylistic criticism to be explicit and systematic, and this involves a description of the metalanguage, the language of criticism itself. If the stylistic critic cannot pretend to be as scientific as the linguist, he can at least attempt to classify the terminology he uses so as to have a fuller comprehension of the workings of language both in the work of art itself and in the process of analysing and evaluating it.

Critical vocabulary may be divided into four main categories: formal terminology, referential content words, descriptive and affective terminology, and classificatory terminology. Each category will be discussed briefly below.

Formal terminology

In literary criticism there is a whole range of words which give us the basic concepts we use and the general framework within which the critic works. These words help to define what art is, what its formal characteristics are, and what categories of description are used both in literary criticism and linguistic analysis. As this class of words is concerned with concepts and formal characteristics we shall call the terms which belong to it *formal terminology*. Formal terms are the very backbone of criticism, the *sine qua non* of the language of criticism, because our evaluation of a work of art and our ability to abstract and talk about it depend on the conceptual framework which the formal terms give us. Formal terms constitute the technical dimension of critical terminology, being free from built-in judgements and free from positive and negative connotations. Under this category we subsume:

1. all the terminology referring to the modes of literature, for instance, fiction, novel, play, poem, epic, sonnet, and so on;
2. the various components and dimensions of a work of art, for instance, character, narrative structure, dialogue, monologue;
3. the determinants of linguistic format, for instance, content, participant, medium;
4. figures of speech and 'devices' for instance, simile, metaphore, personification, alliteration, parallelism, irony;
5. all levels of linguistic description, for instance, sentence, clause, phrase, intonation, rhythm, diction, phoneme, word.

Referential content terminology

Under this category we subsume a whole range of words described by W. K. Wimsatt, to whom we owe the term, as 'the whole vocabulary of referential content'.[22] Literature is about man, society and the universe; it is about man's conflict with man, man's values, man's fight against nature, man's search for perfection and for a better society. The language of literary criticism necessarily includes words referring to man, life, religion, love, culture contact, culture conflict, good and evil, contradictions and their resolutions. This class of words defines the content, the *what* of creative writing. It is at this point, the level of content, that the literary critic most directly shows the interaction between literature and life for here, at the point of intersection between art and life, the critic is not talking about art in terms of art, but about life in terms of art. Here the sociopolitical and socioeconomic aspects of a society, here the political ideology and religious outlook of the writer and those of his society are reflected and evaluated; here the message or meaning of the writer's artistic utterance is discussed and evaluated. Thus in addition to having an artistic quality, literature has a social nature and this social nature is reflected in the critic's language.

Descriptive and affective terminology

Here we are concerned with the quality of a work of art, the characteristics of the writer's style and the effects of the writer's style and technique on the reader. It is possible to split this class of terms into two — 'descriptive terminology', where the focus is on the work of art and on the author's handling of it, and 'affective terminology', where we record the effects of the artistic creation on the reader. This subcategorization stems from a recognition of the fact that evaluative vocabulary in literary criticism is used in relation to points of reference. At one end of the scale the description is directed to the author or the artistic creation itself. Thus we can say Maillu is blunt, vulgar, amusing, humorous or witty. Or we can say Eliot's style is abstract, conceptual and complicated. Milton is said to use an elevated style in *Paradise Lost*. In relation to the various determinants of linguistic format, the style of the writer will, in our scheme of things, be described as appropriate or inappropriate, in character or out of character. In all these cases the focus is on either of two points of reference, the author or the artefact itself. At the other end of the scale the reader constitutes the yardstick by which we measure the success of the author, as the success or failure of a work of art will depend on how an informed readership responds to the author's finished utterance, how experienced readers respond to his various linguistic choices and narrative technique. Thus critics and readers may say that a novel is exciting, compelling, boring or moving. We may say of a book which has a low readability that it is inhibiting — the reader either recoils from it, finds it difficult, or simply gets bored. A book that has a high degree of readability may be said to be appealing, fascinating, bewitching. Here we have gone beyond the description of the quality of the object itself to a consideration of its effects on the reader. The critic recognizes that a work of art can have a psychological effect on the reader; it is 'capable of arousing aesthetic experience' in him.[23] Here the point of reference is the reader, not the artefact or the author. But I hasten to add that the capacity of the work of art to arouse aesthetic experience is dependent on its own qualities, so that in the final analysis we cannot divorce what we might call the 'descriptive aspects' of criticism from the 'affective aspects', as the one depends on the other. It should be understood of course that in talking about descriptive vocabulary we put the main emphasis on the object, on the art-work itself, and not on the author. We could subcategorize descriptive vocabulary into author-oriented terms and object(artefact)-oriented terms, but the distinction is unnecessary and sometimes non-existent. We could say of an author, for example, that so-and-so is vulgar, or we could say so-and-so's style is vulgar. In the first case the criticism is directed against the author, and in the second more against the style than the author himself, but the distinction between author and style is not very important. It doesn't really matter in which way we express ourselves.

It could also be argued that many terms are both object-oriented and reader-oriented. When we say a novel is readable, for instance, we are describing a quality which the novel has and in the same breath giving an account of one of its effects on the reader, for readability is only definable in relation to the reader. The distinction between affective and descriptive vocabulary may therefore appear to be difficult to define in clear-cut terms, but it is certainly there. The distinction emerges partly from the referential orientation of the words employed by the critic and partly from the nature of his emphasis (whether it is on the reader or on the object).

In the category of descriptive and affective terminology, there are some words and concepts used in stylistic criticism which call for a more precise definition than we have so far attempted. Most of these revolve around the term 'readability'.

We have already stated that readability can be measured in terms of low, average or high readability. Of course such expressions as 'very readable' or 'extremely readable' are perfectly in order. Under the same category of readability we will decide whether the style is abstract, conceptual or concrete. A style is abstract if the author tends to express himself in abstract terms. It is conceptual if it is infused with ideas, concepts or if ideological issues tend to dominate the writer's handling of language, theme and plot. T. S. Eliot's style, for instance, is conceptual because his poetry works at the level of ideas, and these ideas are reflected in the writer's mode of expression. The opening lines of *Burnt Norton* can serve as an example of this:

> Time present and time past
> Are both perhaps present in time future
> And time future contained in time past.
> If all time is eternally present
> All time is unredeemable.

The lines are certainly abstract, but here the poet rises above the merely abstract and attempts to grapple with ideas and philosophical issues. Abstractness and conceptuality are therefore not synonymous in our definition, as the one (abstractness) operates purely at the level of linguistic choice, while the other (conceptuality) involves the expression of ideas and concepts which the writer is grappling with in his entire work. A style which is not very abstract and not conceptual may be described as concrete or down to earth in the sense that the author conveys his message not through the discussion of abstract ideas or philosophical issues, but simply through the depiction of episode, character and activity.

A very important concept in stylistic criticism is what we term the 'compelling power' of a novel. A book that is appealing to the reader and that thrills and excites the emotions is said to be fascinating, thrilling, bewitching. As the term 'fascinating' is commonly used, it is proposed here that it be the point of reference in our discussion of compelling power. A book will be said to be very compelling or to have a high compelling power if it captures the reader's attention through the writer's successful manipulation of plot, character and language. There is, in our definition, a qualitative difference between fascination and compelling power. Fascination will be associated with the charm that a book has, a charm that arises from a thrilling story which appeals to the reader in such an irresistible way that he finds it difficult to put it down. Compelling power will be regarded as a force that arises from the writer's ordering of plot, character, theme and language, and from the reader's identification with character and his involvement, not only in the charm of the events told in the story, but in the issues raised by the author. These issues shake the reader's moral being and enable him to emerge from the book, not only with a smile or a feeling of satisfaction at having finished an interesting book, but with a new understanding of life, or at least with a reflection on an aspect of life. Thus fascination will be associated with less challenging literature, and compelling power with more serious artistic creations.

Critics often describe a book or part of it as 'moving'. This is an important concept and deserves mention here particularly because it has a bearing on readability. We talk of a novel or scene as moving when the reader finds himself identifying with a suffering character; when he is moved to pity, either in sympathy with a character or characters in a pitiful situation, or in sympathy with man in general — if the writer is capable of inducing the reader to reflect on the tragic aspects of life as Shakespeare does in his great tragedies, *Lear*, *Othello* and *Hamlet*. A book's ability to move contributes to its readability since the reader who is moved to pity, compassion or fear as a result of a suffering or trapped character, will feel compelled to read on to the end, very often with the hope of seeing the object of his pity saved from the worst. In traditional folktales the solution is of the 'they lived happily ever after' type. The novel is a mainly realistic genre, and rarely offers such simple and wholly pleasing solutions.

Classificatory terminology

Every competent reader of a work of art is likely to express an opinion as to whether the novel or poem he has read is a success or not, and if successful to what extent. Here we are not evaluating minute aspects of the book in isolation, but the whole novel, play or poem in its entirety.

We weigh and balance its virtues and shortcomings and arrive at what we may call 'the sum total of our multifarious response' to the work of art, a response which is the result of the final and overall impression which it leaves on us. We have responded to the artistic creation in various ways and have gone through a multiplicity of aesthetic and psychological experiences, not blindly, but guided by our scale of values, our sensibility and our tools of analysis, and we are now able to sum up our evaluation of the work of art in a word, phrase or sentence such as 'good', 'mediocre', 'great', 'a first-class novel', 'a fine achievement', 'a bad book'. By so doing we are, as it were, ranking a novel, putting it in a class of works of equal or similar value.

The rank of a novel depends on all the variables we have established, that is, its readability, appropriateness, and effectiveness of linguistic choices, its content value and aesthetic quality. The rank of a novel is, however, not absolute as it depends, not on one critic's evaluation, but on the novel's ability to stand up to the tastes of various critics at various times in various lands. A book that has been widely accepted as of artistic excellence becomes a classic. Chinua Achebe's *Things Fall Apart*, for example, has gained worldwide acclaim and could be classified as a classic.

Stylistic Criticism and the Study of Literature

It is a common practice among students of literature in Africa and elsewhere to regard the study of literature as consisting merely in the narration of plots and the discussion of themes and characters, at the expense of the aesthetic aspects of literature. The discussion of 'issues' raised in literary works of art becomes the primary, if not exclusive, concern of the student of literature. Such an approach may lead us into a situation where we are concerned 'solely with the slogan of the day which may be completely forgotten tomorrow'.[24] Today we are shouting, 'Down with imperialism! Down with colonialism!' Tomorrow we will be shouting something else. Now when the political slogan has become irrelevant, the criticism that was based on it will also become irrelevant. Criticism based on sound aesthetic principles will forever be useful. It may be overtaken by a more satisfactory theory but, like Aristotle's *Poetics*, it will form a basis for further developments. A major concern of stylistic criticism is to give due emphasis to the aesthetic aspects of literary works of art. It takes cognizance of the fact that a work of art must be objectively analysed and evaluated in terms of an aesthetically sound set of parameters, and that the student of literature should be trained to take stock of these parameters if his study of literature is to be satisfactory and intellectually challenging.

The aesthetic parameters we are concerned with here are mainly of a linguistic nature, but it is clear that stylistic criticism is not only confined to what is conventionally called 'style' in literature, 'the occasional linguistic idiosyncracies which characterise an individual's uniqueness'.[25] We are not merely concerned with what is idiosyncratic about a writer, but equally with the *effect* of his manner of presentation, and with the relationship between language and content. Our discussion of such variables as readability and point of view will compel us to include the narrative structure in our analysis of fiction, though the focus will always be on the linguistic format.

But it must be emphasized that stylistic criticism is not merely concerned with aesthetic and formal aspects of fiction. It does not disregard the political, social and moral issues raised in contemporary literature. This is where it parts company with literary stylistics and the traditional approach to the study of style which tend to be concerned with the linguistic format to the exclusion of content. Our focus on the linguistic format will lead us to a greater understanding of content and character, and in our evaluation criteria we regard the content value as a major variable contributing to the overall quality of a work of fiction. What this leads to is a recognition of the fact that sociological and aesthetic issues are of equal importance in literary criticism. We put emphasis on the aesthetic and formal dimensions of fiction only to discover how social, ideological and moral issues are discussed and given substance *in an artistic way* in genuine works of art.

Notes

1   R. Crane, *The Languages of Criticism and the Structure of Poetry*, p. 115.
2   *The Appropriate Form.*
3   *What is a Novel?* and *Possibilities.*
4   *The Anatomy of the Novel.*
5   *The Novel: Modern Essays in Criticism.*
6   See Fowler's essay in M. Bradbury and D. Palmer (1970) Stratford-upon-Avon Studies 12: *Contemporary Criticism*, p. 186.
7   *The Necessity of Art*, p. 152, and p. 151.
8   What Ayi Kwei Armah says on this subject is relevant here. See his article 'Larsony or Fiction as Criticism of Fiction', *New Classic*, No. 4.
9   See 'An Approach to the Study of Style' in D. C. Freeman (1970) *Linguistics and Literary Style*, Holt, Rinehart & Winston, Inc. See also Enkvist, Spencer and Gregory (1964) *Linguistics and Style.*
10 See M. Bradbury, *What is a Novel?*, p. 4.
11 *The Forsaken Lover*, p. 41.
12 *Morning Yet on Creation Day*, pp. 61–2.
13 See T. S. Dorsch, *Classical Literary Criticism*, p. 41.
14 See Enkvist, Spencer and Gregory, *Linguistics and Style*, p. 89.
15 Eliot, *The Sacred Wood*, p. 100.
16 I. A. Richards, *Principles of Literary Criticism*, p. 19.
17 Fischer, *The Nevessity of Art*, p. 9.
18 Elliot, op. cit., p. 58.
19 Ibid., p. 53.

20   Fischer, op. cit., p. 131.
21   See T. Eagleton, *Marxism and Literary Criticism*, p. 24ff.
22   See D. Lodge, *Language of Fiction*, p. 70.
23   Wellek and Warren, *Theory of Literature*, p. 241.
24   G. Lukács, *Studies in European Realism*, p. 125.
25   See Crystal and Davy, *Investigating English Style*, p. 9.

Part Two

Practical Analysis of Novels

4 Gabriel Okara — *The Voice*

▼▼▼▼▼▼▼▼▼▼▼▼▼▼▼▼▼▼▼▼▼▼▼▼▼▼▼▼▼

Okara's Unconventional English

Much has been said about the language and theme of Okara's novel, *The Voice*. Critics have noted that it is a moral and/or political allegory which takes the form of a quest.[1] The story is told in the third person with the author as narrator. *The Voice* is thus constructed differently from Tutuola's *The Palm-Wine Drinkard*, which is told in the first person by the hero. *The Voice* is a realistic novel while *The Palm-Wine Drinkard* is a romance and belongs to fantasy fiction. But the quest structure in both novels is basically the same. In both the hero goes away and at some stage comes back with a deeper insight into the nature of human life.

Again, in *The Voice*, as in *The Palm-Wine Drinkard*, linguistic idiosyncrasies are very outstanding. In fact the very first thing that strikes the reader is the strangeness of Okara's sentence structures and idioms. This can be demonstrated by a close analysis of part of the first chapter, which opens with the following words:

> Some of the townsmen said Okolo's eyes were not right, his head was not correct. This they said was the result of his knowing too much book, walking too much in the bush, and others said it was due to his staying too long alone by the river.
>
> So the town of Amatu talked and whispered; so the world talked and whispered. Okolo had no chest, they said. His chest was not strong and he had no shadow. Everything in this world that spoiled a man's name they said of him, all because he had dared to search for *it*. He was in search of *it* with all his inside and with all his shadow.   (p. 23)

Linguistic peculiarities are obvious here: 'Okolo's eyes were not right', 'his head was not correct'. This we are told, was the result of 'knowing too much book'. The simplicity and un-Englishness of the language is what the reader notices first. In the first paragraph, Okara's language sounds like the English of a schoolboy who has not yet mastered the language. Another feature that strikes the reader in the opening paragraph is the device of repetition. The repitition of 'too much' and its variant 'too long' has something of nursery rhymes about it. One is reminded of the rhythm and simplicity of many African traditional songs.

In the first sentence of the second paragraph, the repetition of 'so', 'talked', 'whispered', and the syntactic structure of the sentence give rise to rhythms typical of traditional songs. It has been said that Okara makes use of the idiom of his mother tongue, Ijaw, and no doubt they are the rhythms of Ijaw that we feel here. But there is something in Okara's technique that echoes the rhythms of other African languages as well. The rhythm of the sentence under discussion could have come from a traditional song of the Shona people of Zimbabwe.

In the second paragraph there is one Ijaw idiom after another: Okolo's critics said he 'had no chest'; they said he 'had no shadow'. In the same paragraph Okara also reveals his technique of talking about something without referring to it by a specific name: 'He was in search of *it* with all his inside and with all his shadow.' Okolo's search for *it* is what is going to occupy us throughout the length of the book. The think itself is nameless and so we have to read on until we discover what *it* is. What we see now is that the search for *it* is a cause for much concern among the people of Amatu. While Okolo is busy searching for *it*, the people of Amatu are criticizing him for the search and seem to be so worried that they want him to stop the search:

> Why should Okolo look for *it*, they wondered. Things have changed, the world has turned and they are now the Elders. No one in the past has asked for *it*. Why should Okolo expect to find *it* now that they are the Elders? No, he must stop his search. He must not spoil their pleasure.   (p. 24)

The question and comment structure of the passage shows something of the anxiety of the Elders. We now see that Okolo is doing something that was never done before. He is presenting a challenge that has never been presented before, and those who are disturbed by this challenge are the Elders (note the capital E) who are *now* the Elders. This clearly indicates that Okolo is challenging African political leaders after independence. The author chooses to portray the leaders as Chiefs. This is in agreement with what happened in some African countries such as Nigeria and Lesotho, where chiefs still exercised power after independence. Thus a chief like Izongo could be seen to stand for a regional traditional leader, while the Big One of Sologa represents the national leader in, say, Lagos.

The African and traditional context in which most of the events in the book took place is clearly reflected in the passage which depicts the messengers talking to one another. The field of discourse reflects traditional thinking and the preoccupations of the traditional mind:

> First messenger: 'My right foot has hit against a stone.'
> Second messenger: 'Is it good or bad?'
> First messenger (*solemnly*): 'It's bad.'   (p. 24)

We see in the rest of the passage that the first messenger and the second

messenger represent traditional beliefs and superstitions. If a foot hits
something, it is a warning that something will happen. The third
messenger, who has passed Standard Six, regards these superstitions
with contempt and responds 'nonsense'. There is in this passage a
conflict between the educated and the uneducated.

From a stylistic point of view this passage demonstrates one of the
techniques used in the book: the depiction of scenes as if in a play.
Devices typical of a play are used, such as the interlocutors' names or
titles appearing at the beginning of each utterance, and many of the
utterances are accompanied by typical stage directions, for example,
(*With contempt*), (*Spits on the ground*). (*Angrily*), (*Raising his voice*), etc.

With this conversation we are taken to Okolo's house. Here is
another passage from this section of the book to illustrate another aspect
of Okara's English:

> Shuffling feet turned Okolo's head to the door. He saw three men
> standing silent, opening not their mouths. 'Who are you people
> be?' Okolo asked. The people opened not their mouths. 'If you are
> coming-in people be, then come in.' The people opened not their
> mouths. 'Who are you?' Okolo again asked, walking to the men. As
> Okolo closer to the men walked, the men quickly turned and ran
> out.   (pp. 26–7)

One of the significant features in this passage is the inversion of word
order as exemplified in the expression 'opening not their mouths' and
'opened not their mouths'. The repetition of this structure gives the
passage a biblical ring. The sentences could have come from the
Authorized Version of the Bible. On the other hand there are structures
which cannot be related to anything written in Standard English,
whether modern or archaic. Among these is the use of *be* at the end of
questions and sentences: 'Who are you people be?' 'If you are coming-in
people be, then come in.' 'Be' like 'his inside' is a frequent feature of the
book. It occurs, for example on p. 72: 'A stinking thing like a rotten
corpse be', 'for it is a strong thing be to send away one who is looking for
it.'

An excellent example of the repeated inversion of word order occurs at
the beginning of Chapter 8. The girl whom Okolo protected from cold
weather is being charged with having had physical contact with him:

> The daughter-in-law her hands clasping and unclasping opened
> not her mouth, standing in the centre of a circle of men and women.
> Her husband, sitting opposite her, opened not his mouth; the
> mother-in-law, sitting near her son, opened not her mouth but with
> words moving up her throat she her lips tightened and the
> imprisoned words creased her brows and made her breath like a
> running person's. The men were palmwine and beer drinking,
> palmwine and beer bought by the son of the mother-in-law, for it

was he who called them on his mother's teaching words to find out
the truth from his bride and to invoke things of the ground, if she
spoke things that did not enter their insides.   (p. 101)

Here the rhythm is very close to the rhythm of nursery rhymes and folk-
tales.

Poetic Qualities

Though written in simple language, *The Voice* has an unmistakable
poetic quality which is evident from the very first chapter. The following
passage depicts Okolo's impressions of the crowd that has been chasing
him — he is now in Tuere's hut:

> Faces, a mass of faces glistening with sweat in the moonlight stood,
> talking, arguing. Grim faces like the dark mysterious forest afire
> with flies. Then a shadow blocked his view, then silence. And a
> voice clear and cool like a glass of water, from the standing shadow
> sallied forth.   (p. 28)

Such a passage is striking for its use of imagery and alliteration. The
alliteration consists in the repetition of such sounds as the fricatives *s* and
f, the hard voiced plosive *g* and the hard metallic voiceless sound *k*, as in
'clear' and 'cool'. The imagery is effective both from its alliteration and
from its powerful visual sense, 'the dark mysterious forest afire with flies';
'a mass of faces glistening with sweat'. With the simile 'a voice clear and
cool like a glass of water', the beauty of the speaker's voice is evoked by
the reference to a glass of clear and cool water.

Perhaps the most poetic passage in the chapter is the one which
describes the darkness in Tuere's hut after she has frightened the crowd
away. Okolo is with her in the hut:

> Presently, Tuere stepped silently in and put the mat over the door.
> And the hut became dark with darkness exceeding darkness.
> Though they were only a few paces apart, Okolo could not see her.
> They stood thus silent without each other seeing, listening to their
> insides, listening to the darkness. Then suddenly Okolo heard
> walking feet. Feet walking towards the dying embers at the hearth.
> Then he saw the embers move and glow like a new-appearing sun
> or a going-down sun. Then he saw splinters of firewood drop on
> the embers. And then he heard her trying to blow the embers to
> living flames. She blew, blew, blew and blew, but the embers only
> glowed not responding like a god more sacrifice demanding. They
> only glowed showing a face intent in supplication. She continued
> to blow, her breath coming in soft gusts. Then a token flame shot
> up momentarily and died.   (pp. 32–3)

The darkness of the room is first described in the second sentence, where the iteration of 'dark' and 'darkness' introduces us to the unimaginable darkness that unfolds as we read further. The darkness enveloping the room is further described by showing how, though they were very close to each other, Tuere and Okolo could not see each other, as they stood 'listening to their insides' and 'listening to the darkness'. Because he could not see, Okolo 'heard' Tuere only as 'walking feet'. As we read on, we find the image of darkness being contrasted with images relating to fire and light. Such images come out in the use of words like 'embers', 'glow', 'sun', 'flames', 'blow'.

The role and effort of Tuera is very significant. It is she who 'blew, blew, blew and blew' without at first getting any more than glowing embers. It is she who goes on blowing, tired though she is, until we are told: 'Then a token flame shot up momentarily and died.' The darkness described here is not simply darkness, it is symbolic darkness; darkness symbolizing the evils surrounding Tuere and Okolo, the darkness of a world which rejoices in corruption and does not want to face the truth of social and spiritual change. Tuere is thus struggling to bring some light to this dark world of thoughtless Elders and savage crowds. She is thus *lux in tenebris*, 'light in darkness'. She and Okolo together are symbolic of the forces of the light of truth and social justice. Those who fight for truth and justice are not completely disappointed. Their efforts are repaid. In the same way, Tuere's efforts in trying to produce a flame in darkness are brought to fruition — with the help of Okolo:

> As he moved back unseen hands took the firewood from his hands and crossed them on the embers. Then there were more blowings. Then suddenly a twin flame shot up. The twin flame going into one another and becoming one, grew long and short, spread, twisted and danced, devouring the essence of the firewood like passion. And the face of Tuere was satisfaction, for her breath and shadow had gone into the flame.   (p. 33)

There is here an attempt not only to present a beautiful visual image of fire, but also to capture the essence of fire and by suggestion, the victory of light over darkness. The twin flame shoots up with beauty past the description of beauty, and we notice that Tuere is filled with satisfaction when she sees the fruits of her labours. We also notice that the beauty of the flame is reflected in a subtle manner on Tuere's own face:

> She remained kneeling before the dancing flame with face intent, looking at the flame, looking at what is behind the flame, the root of the flame.   (p. 33)

These words have more meaning than meets the eye. On one level 'the root of the flame' may be taken to refer to firewood, but on a deeper level it refers to the source of light, the source of the light of truth. Tuere is therefore contemplating on the nature of true meaning in life. That is why before Okolo can say anything she goes straight to the subject of his search, *it*: 'How do you expect to find it? How do you expect to find *it* when everybody has locked up his inside?' Tuere is able to go to 'the bottom of things' when the darkness around her has been dispelled by the light of the flame she has successfully kindled. Her own shadow, we are told, 'had gone into the flame' — it had been devoured by the light of the fire.

At times, Okara heightens the poetic quality of his prose by again using the rhythms of traditional songs, referred to in the previous section. This occurs in the following passage which depicts the torture of Okolo by Izongo's men:

> The people snapped at him like hungry dogs snapping at bones. They carried him in silence like the silence of ants carrying a crumb of yam or fishbone. Then they put him down and dragged him past thatch houses that in the dark looked like pigs with their snouts in the ground; pushed and dragged him past mud walls with pitying eyes; pushed and dragged him past concrete walls with concrete eyes; pushed and dragged him along the waterside like soldier ants with their prisoner. They pushed and dragged him in panting silence, shuffling silence, broken only by an owl hooting from the darkness of the orange tree in front of Chief Izongo's house.   (pp. 38–9)

The rhythm resulting from the repetition of 'pushed and dragged him' is obvious. But the poetry is not only in the rhythm but also in the imagery. The emphasis is on animal images suggesting the inhuman treatment of Okolo by the savage crowds. There are a good number of similes referring to animals: 'The people snapped at him like hungry dogs snapping at bones'; 'they carried him in silence like the silence of ants carrying a crumb of yam or fish bone'; they dragged him past houses that in the dark looked like pigs with their snouts in the ground'; 'they pushed and dragged him like soldier ants with their prisoner'.

As a result of this treatment Okolo gets physically tired, but at first his mind is quite clear, so clear that he describes the hatred surrounding him in highly poetic language:

> I am moving round and round caught in a whirlpool of hate and greed and I smell the smell of hate in their sweat glistening on their backs ...   (p. 39)

The fifth chapter provides us with some of the most poetic passages in the whole novel, when Okolo's experiences as he arrives in Sologa of the Big One are recounted. This is how the writer expresses the intensity of the darkness into which Okolo moves as he steps from the canoe:

> The voice chuckled and said: 'We are taking you to a place where you can find *it*.' As this two chunks of darkness detached themselves from the darkness and gripped Okolo's hands and

pushed him through the black black night like the back of a cooking pot.

Through the black black night Okolo walked, stumbled, walked. His inside was a room with chairs, cushions, papers scattered all over the floor by thieves. Okolo walked, stumbled, walked. His eyes shut and opened, shut and opened, expecting to see a light in each opening, but none he saw in the black black night.

At last the black black night like the back of a cooking pot entered his inside and grabbing his thoughts, threw them out into the blacker than black night. And Okolo walked, stumbled, walked with an inside empty of thoughts except the black black night.   (p. 76)

In this passage Okara uses a number of interesting devices. One is the concretization of insubstantial things. The expression 'two chunks of darkness detached themselves' not only evokes fear and an eerie feeling, but also has the effect of making us imagine darkness as something massive and solid. These two chunks probably stand for two people (or two hands) but so dark is it that the two people can only be seen as part of the frightening and overwhelming darkness surrounding Okolo, the darkness of the back of a cooking pot. It is not only the night that is objectified, but also his mind and his thoughts. He is in a confused state of mind, but Okara does not use direct referential language to express this. The confusion is described in terms of a room 'with chairs, cushions, papers scattered all over the floor by thieves' — presumably these are spiritual and moral thieves, those who steal his mind, his inside, from him. The concretization of insubstantial things is accompanied by a form of dramatization which makes the author's description vivid and memorable. Okolo's inability to think in the dark night is expressed in terms of a black night that 'entered his inside and grabbing his thoughts, threw them out into the blacker than black night'. Thus short of becoming unconscious Okolo is completely blank in his mind. When he becomes himself again, he finds himself lying on a very cold floor. As he gains consciousness, his thoughts begin 'to fly in his inside darkness like frightened birds hither, thither, homeless' — another expression of confusion.

Apart from this device of dramatization and the concretization of immaterial things, Okara also uses repetition as in 'walked, stumbled, walked'. This device, very commonly used in *The Voice*, sometimes has a beautiful lyrical effect, as in the following example from the same chapter: 'Okolo walked passing eyes, walked passing eyes, walked passing eyes until hunger held him' (p. 80).

Atmosphere and the Dramatic Element in Okara

The poetic qualities of *The Voice* will be fully appreciated if related to other aesthetic qualities of the book. I refer in particular to the dramatic element in the novel and to Okara's evocation of atmosphere.

The strong dramatic element can be demonstrated initially by quoting the passage where Izongo's messengers are trying to arrest Okolo:

> Okolo seeing the messengers, recognised them and questioned them. But the men, in spite of their grim faces, opened not their mouths. The remaining crowd hushed. The silence passed silence. The three messengers faced Okolo, opening not their mouths. A man from the back of the crowd pushed his way to the messengers. The four of them put their heads together while with their eyes they looked at Okolo. They put their heads together for awhile and walked towards Okolo, as if stalking an animal. And Okolo stood looking. They moved nearer. Okolo stood. They moved nearer and suddenly, pounced on Okolo.   (p. 27)

The language here is powerful and evocative. It presents such visual pictures to the mind as that of four men putting their heads together. The author enables the reader to participate in Okolo's fears here: 'They put their heads together for awhile and walked towards Okolo, as if stalking an animal. And Okolo stood …'

The idea of 'stalking an animal' is particularly fear-inspiring. And the short sentences which follow, showing Okolo standing while the danger of the four men moves nearer and nearer, are very dramatic. The repetition of 'they moved nearer' and 'Okolo stood' has the effect of making us momentarily held in fearful suspense; but only momentarily — the writer does not sustain the suspense for long before he allows the messengers to 'pounce on Okolo'. The manner in which the four men hold him is most powerfully described:

> Hands clawed at him, a thousand hands, the hands of the world. Okolo twisted, struggled and kicked with all his shadow, with all his life and to his astonishment, he saw himself standing free.
> (pp. 27–8)

The image of hands 'clawing' like paws of animals, and the idea of Okolo twisting and struggling and kicking 'with all his shadow' is beautiful, powerful language. The 'thousand hands' are symbolic. These are the hands of the multitude of people who are opposed to Okolo's search for *it*. They are indeed 'the hands of the world', not just the hands of the messengers, not just the hands of the people outside Okolo's house.

The next group of sentences centre around the action of running. Again the writer uses the technique of repetition, repeating the word 'ran' in its various forms; and to heighten further the drama of Okolo's escape, he contrasts long and short sentences so that the short ones refer to Okolo and the long ones to the people chasing him:

> He ran. Running feet followed him. He ran. A million pursuing feet thundered after him.   (p. 28)

We also notice that here the pronoun 'he' is used. In many parts of the novel 'Okolo' is reiterated until it rings like a bell in the reader's mind, as in the following passage from Chapter 5:

> Okolo ran and the light also ran. Okolo ran, the light ran. Okolo ran and hit a wall with his head. Okolo looked and the light was no more.   (p. 77)

It is not just the repetition of the words 'Okolo' and 'light' that is significant here, but also the alternation of these words. They have the effect of presenting simultaneously in our minds both the victim of the danger, Okolo, and the source of his fear, the strange light. We participate in his tension and psychological experiences — the fear that he feels, the fear of being confused and wanting to hold onto something that can make him see and understand things — the light — but failing to achieve anything. Thus apart from enabling him to present the events in a dramatic way, Okara's technique also helps him to create the atmosphere of fear and eerieness whose effect, as Obiechina observes, is that of a 'nightmare'.[2] A good example of this is the incident first described — from Chapter 2 — where Okolo becomes unconscious after being tortured by Izongo's men:

> A fly stood on his nose. Okolo turned on his side and continued to sleep. Another stood on his ear. He shook his head. It flew off and stood on the ear. He turned and slept on his back. The fly stood on his eyes. He shook his head. The fly flew off. He was now between sleeping and waking, thinking and not thinking, floating between sky and earth. The fly settled on his mouth. He tried to move his hand but his hand would not move! Then suddenly fear opened his eyes wide, in spite of his strong chest, and he came down to earth. And as he gazed at the ceiling, he saw yesterday's night passing before his eyes. Okolo shut his eyes to shut off the nightmare and spoke with his inside ...   (p. 39)

In this passage we see again the device discussed above, that of the dramatic alternation of sentences referring to Okolo as a victim and sentences referring to the source of his fear or discomfort, in this case the troublesome fly. We get flashes turning our minds alternately to Okolo and to the object, to Okolo and to the object, as if in a film. That Okolo has been unconscious is shown in the sentence: 'He was now between sleeping and waking, thinking and not thinking, floating between sky and earth'. As he begins to gain consciousness he discovers that he cannot move his hand. This is the function of the fly — to bring him to a

shocking awareness of his own predicament. Okolo wants to chase the
fly away and in that process he discovers, much to his horror, that he is
bound with a rope. The discovery throws him into a fit of fear which
brings back the horror of last night's experiences in the form of an
unbearable nightmare. Okara is thus using the nightmarish effect on two
planes: the atmosphere in which the events take place is itself
nightmarish, but as if that is not sufficient, Okara creates an actual
nightmare before us by making Okolo aware of his own nightmare:
'Okolo shut his eyes to shut off the nightmare ...'

When Okolo arrives in Sologa, in Chapter 5, he finds the atmosphere
full of fear and strange things. No sooner has he stepped out of the canoe
to touch the soil of Sologa than he hears an ominous voice advising him
not to know 'the bottom of things' and informing him, 'we are taking you
to a place where you can find *it*' (p. 76). Later he finds himself in a very
dark room where the atmosphere is more nightmarish and alarming
than anywhere else. Okolo simply has no idea where he is, who brought
him here, where next to go. His experiences in Amatu might have been
better because he better understood the circumstances in which he was
arrested. He remembered Izongo and his people coming to fetch him
from Tuere's hut. But here, where there is a cold floor and rock-like
darkness, here where he sees a strange light in total darkness, Okolo is
utterly confused and thoroughly afraid:

> Okolo for years and years lay on the cold cold floor at the rock-like
> darkness staring. Then suddenly he saw a light. He drew his feet
> with all his soul and his feet came. He drew his hands and his hands
> came. He stood up with eyes on the light and walked towards the
> light. As he moved towards the light, the light also moved back. He
> moved faster the light also moved faster back. Okolo ran and the
> light also ran. Okolo ran, the light ran. Okolo ran and hit a wall
> with his head. Okolo looked and the light was no more. He then
> stretched his hands forth and touched the wall. His fingers felt
> dents and holes. Okolo walked sideways like a crab with his fingers
> on the wall, feeling dents and holes, dents and holes in the rock-like
> darkness until his feet struck an object. As Okolo stopped and felt
> the object, his body became cold. His heartbeat echoed in the rock-
> like darkness and his head expanded. Still, he felt along the object
> until his fingers went into two holes. As his fingers went into the
> holes he quickly withdrew them and ran. He ran and fell, ran and
> fell over the objects...   (p. 77)

The dramatic element here is strong. It is used to present a striking
contrast between light and darkness. There is a mysteriousness about the
moving light. There is something overpoweringly weird and horrifying
about the place. Is the light meant to be a glimpse of the light outside this
strange building? Probably. But it may be taken to have a double
reference. It refers to the light outside this horrid room, the light which

Okolo is anxious to see but cannot see; it also refers to spiritual light. Okolo is looking for light; he is searching for *it*, but he cannot find it here in Sologa. To Okolo in his present situation, however, the light may also appear to be something frightening.

The images which the author uses are deliberately calculated to cause horror and strike fear down the spine of the reader. Thus Okolo walks sideways 'like a crab', and the very rhythm of the sentence is meant to reflect the movements and shape of that strange aquatic creature: 'Okolo walked sideways like a crab with his fingers on the wall, feeling dents and holes, dents and holes in the rock-like darkness until his feet struck an object.' The object sends a shiver down Okolo's spine. His body becomes cold, his heart pounds as a result of fear, his hair stands on end, or, to use the writer's own expressive image, 'his head expanded'. He realizes to his horror that there are human bones in this place, but the author does not tell us directly here that these strange objects which Okolo feels are human bones. We get the information when Okolo is reporting to the policeman, on p. 79: 'Yes, people dragged me away and put me in the dark room, with bones like ...', and later 'with bones like human ...'. Perhaps he wants to say the bones feel like human skeletons. It is certain however that the holes in the bones are what really terrify Okolo: 'As his fingers went into the holes he quickly withdrew them and ran. He ran and fell, ran and fell over other objects ...'

The writer's withdrawal of information is quite significant here. He does not want to explain what the light which Okolo sees really is, he does not want to tell us what the objects, which Okolo feels, really are. This withdrawal of information heightens the drama in a subtle way by surrounding the objects with something of a mystery.

From the darkness of this mysterious place Okolo is suddenly thrown into the humdrum of city life in Sologa. Here the events take place in broad daylight, but the dreamlike atmosphere is still there:

> Okolo found himself standing in daylight in a street, hither and thither turning his eyes. He stood turning his eyes this way and that way in the street. Thus he stood with the crowd passing him by: cars honking, people shouting, people dying, women delivering, beggars begging for alms, people feasting, people crying, people laughing, politicians with grins that do not reach their insides begging for votes, priests building houses, people doubting, people marrying, people divorcing, priests turning away worshippers, people hoping, hopes breaking platelike on cement floors.
> (pp. 77–8)

Here we get a full picture of the diversity of life in Sologa. In one powerful sentence Okara has presented a fantastic picture of human activity and human suffering, so that Sologa becomes a miscrocosmic reflection of the human condition in general. The numbers of people involved here must be very large indeed, and Amatu must appear a very small village in the eyes of Okolo compared with this massive city. Life is seen in a dreamlike fashion, and Okolo's view of Sologa is like the vision of Piers the Plowman who falls asleep and sees a field full of all manner of people — farmers, rich people, slanderers, beggars, sinful hermits and their harlots, friars and covetous cheats.[3] A striking feature of the passage is the repetition of present participals of verbs which has a cumulative effect, while the last clause gives us another example of the author's technique of concretizing ideas and immaterial things: 'hopes breaking platelike on cement floors'. It also has a power and finality that symbolizes in vivid terms the hopelessness of Okolo's search. He came to Sologa with hope; he will leave it frustrated, his hopes having broken 'platelike on cement floors'. The hopelessness of Okolo's search can be seen from what immediately follows. As he stands watching this confused crowd of humans from all walks of life, Okolo sees a policeman to whom he reports what happened to him last night. This 'law man' does not even want to hear the truth about Okolo's experiences in the dark room with human bones, because if he does anything against the Big One of Sologa then even the law won't protect him. So, after telling Okolo that he will investigate, he chews the piece of paper on which he wrote the statement and 'went to a bar and washed it down with a beer!' (p. 80).

Character and Language in *The Voice*

Yet another striking aspect of Okara's style in *The Voice* is the way in which language is related to character. In Chapter 2 three of the major characters in the book — Izongo, Okolo and Abadi — are involved in a debate. We notice here that while Okolo is morally a free person, the Elders are puppets of Izongo. Izongo capriciously orders the Elders: 'Laugh!' and they bare their teeth making a noise 'that could hardly pass for laughter'. The Elders have no will of their own. Their role is amply defined by their chief spokesman, Abadi, the man of education who boasts about degrees obtained from the three major western capitalist countries — England, America and Germany (pp. 43–4).

The first thing to note about Abadi's language is that, unlike that of Izongo and other characters, his English is good Standard English, reflecting native English idioms, not expressions translated from the local language. The second thing to notice is that Abadi's language is that of typical political propaganda and slogans. Expressions like 'honourable leader', 'momentous decisions', 'imperialists', and 'toe the party line' punctuate his utterances. In politics, words are twisted to suit the aims and wishes of those who control power, and those who control power usually have their henchmen to spread their propaganda for them. Thus in George Orwell's *Animal Farm* we find the dictator Napoleon using the eloquent speaker, Squealer, as his spokesman. In *The Voice* Izongo has a good spokesman in the highly educated Abadi to resist the challenge presented by Okolo, who has no more than secondary education, and to channel the thinking of all the citizens of

Amatu towards an acceptance of what Izongo stands for. Abadi is well versed in the language of politics: 'So you and I know what is expected of us, and that is, we must toe the party line. We must have discipline and self-sacrifice in order to see this fight through to its logical conclusion' (p. 43). The word-twisting and mind-twisting goes on: 'Our duty, therefore, is clear. We must support our most honourable leader' (p. 43). To sound more convincing Abadi there and then declares his 'most loyal and unswerving support' and even pledges his 'very blood' to the cause.

Like many conservative and reactionary political leaders in Africa, Abadi knows how to pose as a revolutionary, denouncing 'imperialism' and using the language of the socialist ideology:

> You and I are comrades in arms and we must see this thing through
> to its logical conclusion. So let us with one voice answer the
> question that our leader has put before us a short while ago. We are
> in a democracy and everyone has the right to express any opinion.
> But we have to think what our leader has done for us.   (p. 45)

While the first sentence quoted here employs revolutionary language, the rest of the extract shows the complete twisting of logic that is a common feature of political speeches. There is a contradiction in what Abadi says. This contradiction is shown in the contrast between the last two sentences. The ideals of democracy and the freedom of expression which goes with democracy are completely nullified by his insistence on the need 'to think what our leader has done for us'. There is no democracy, no freedom of expression, unless the speaker acts and speaks in accordance with the will and wishes of Izongo.

Encouraged by the words of 'the highest son of Amatu' and by the applause he receives from the audience, Izongo himself stands up to speak, and the author makes it a point to inform the reader that the chief is speaking in the vernacular. Using idioms of the people such as 'the spoken words', 'entered our ears', 'my inside', 'my chest', Izongo talks like a father to his little children — his tenor of discourse is a patronizing one: 'Everybody forgets things even myself (when convenient) especially as we have taken much palmwine. Even I, Chief Izongo, who you think knows everything, forgets things' (p. 46).

What he is doing is to reiterate what Abadi has just said, namely that there should be no opposition to him. There should be 'no different voice'. 'All the voices must be one', he says, and goes on to quote Abadi's expression that the people of Amatu have 'a "collective responsibility"'. But unlike Abadi, Izongo does not seek to appeal to the people, he threatens them: 'Anyone who raises not his hand I know is not one of us' (p. 46).

Although he is educated, Okolo does not use the white man's language, when talking to his own people. He uses an English which echoes the language of the people's fathers and thus demonstrates, even in the language he speaks, that he wants to preserve the good traditions of his people:

Our fathers' insides always contained things straight. They did straight things. Our insides were also clean and we did the straight things until the new time came. We can still sweep the dirt out of our houses every morning.   (p. 50)

Thus Izongo cannot accuse Okolo of being proud of western education. Abadi indeed claims that Okolo is speaking as he does 'because he attended a secondary school and thinks he is educated', but that is definitely not the case. While Abadi has book learning with a chain of degrees after his name, while he has attended the best universities in the three major western industrial countries, Okolo has used what little education he has to acquire real knowledge about his society and its predicament. He has acquired an education which has shown him how the values of Amatu's ancestors have been thrown to the dogs, how the influence of western materialism has robbed his people of spiritual values as well as the values embodied in their own language and traditions, and his sole fight is to regain these lost values.

When talking to native speakers of English, however, Okolo speaks good Standard English. In the following passage he is talking to a white man in Sologa:

'You speak English, of course?'
'Yes,' answered Okolo.
'You want to see the Big One?'
'Yes.'
'What about?'
'I want to ask him if he's got *it*.'
'Have you ever heard of the word psychiatrist?'
'Yes.'
'Do you know what a psychiatrist does?'
'Yes.'
'Have you consulted one?'
'No.'
'Why not?'
'Because I do not need his services.'
'I think you need the services of one badly.'
'Why?'
'Because I think you are going mental.'
'Going mental?' Okolo repeated slowly.
'Yes, you are going mental.'
'Why do you think I am going mental? Is it because I am searching for *it*. I thought you would understand,' Okolo said almost pleadingly.
'I am just trying to be helpful.'
'Trying to helpful? You can only be helpful by taking me to the Big One.'   (pp. 86–7)

This is perfectly good and 'educated' English, indicating that Okolo's use of African idioms and syntactic structures is no indication of his inability to speak Standard English. Thus Okolo uses the language appropriate to the situation. When talking to his own people he uses his own language; when talking to Englishmen he speaks the Englishman's language, and does so well. Okolo shows the linguistic flexibility that is demanded of educated people in Africa.

When left to himself, however, he 'thinks in' his own language. As soon as the white man leaves him we find him employing Ijaw modes of expression:

> So he sat on a bench along one forbidding wall of the room and waited, speaking with his inside, thinking of the proverb of his people, the Ijaws, which says, 'If you roast a bird of the air before a fowl, the fowl's head aches'. So his inside many questions asked. Faith and faithlessness adding up to nothing ... man has no more shadow, trees have no more shadow ...   (p. 89)

Another interesting point to note in this novel is the relationship between the author and the main characters. The author is here an omniscient narrator. Okara gives himself the freedom to enter Okolo's mind and record for us what Okolo thinks in different situations. This is in fact how we see the progress of Okolo's spiritual search. We see it through his internal monologue which the author recounts at every stage. At the end of Chapter 5, for example, we see the author narrating Okolo's internal conflict after the failure of his Sologa mission: 'One voice said he should to the asylum go... Another voice said no, he should find a way to go back home...' And this is how we learn that Okolo eventually decides to go home and plant the revolutionary spirit among the masses. He has realized that revolutions are not waged by those in the upper echelons of society; revolutions do not start with the haves, but with the have-nots:

> So, in the end, Okolo said he must to his village return, if he could. But this time he would the masses ask and not Izongo and his Elders. If the masses haven't got *it*, he will create *it* in their insides. He will plant *it*, make *it* grow in spite of Izongo's destroying words.   (p. 90)

There are times when the narrator and the character Okolo almost merge and become indistinguishable one from the other. In such passages, the author is still using the third person, but such indicators of reported speech as 'he said' and 'he thought' do not appear. The narration becomes that of the stream-of-consciousness novel, or the interior monologue, where the focus is on recording and analysing mental states. This is exemplified by the crucial tenth chapter where the *it* is now defined as 'the meaning of life'. One paragraph will do:

Yes, each one has a meaning of life to himself. And that is perhaps
the root of the conflict. No one can enter another's inside. You try
to enter and you are kicked out at the door. You allow another to
enter your inside and see everything in it, you are regarded as one
without a chest or one who nothing knows ... Maybe he is wrong.
There may be only one meaning in life and everybody is just
groping along in their various ways to achieve it like religion —
Christians, Moslems, Animists — all trying to reach God in their
various ways. What is he himself trying to reach? For him it has no
name. Names bring divisions and divisions, strife. So let it be
without a name; let it be nameless ...   (pp. 111–12)

In passages like this the distance between the author and the character
becomes very narrow indeed. What Okolo thinks is a reflection of
Okara's own thoughts. There seems no doubt that here the author
means us to think and reflect on the significance of Okolo's words.

In fact this close relationship between Okara and Okolo is operative
throughout the book. We have noted above that when on his own and
when talking to his fellow countrymen, Okolo uses Ijaw. And it is
Okolo's type of language that Okara takes as the norm in his narrative
passages. He does not take Standard English as the norm from which to
diverge into different styles and directions for the speech of his characters
as demanded by their varied linguistic backgrounds. His norm is
Okolo's 'Ijaw English'. Okara has declared that he believes in using
African ideas and African idioms in his writings, that 'a writer can use the
idioms of his own language in a way that is understandable in English'. 'If
he uses their English equivalents', Okara says, 'he would not be
expressing African ideas and thoughts, but English ones'.[4]

Theme and Symbolism: *The Voice* and the Bible

The theme of *The Voice* can be simply summarized as Okolo's search for
it. Okolo comes nearest to an understanding of *it* in Chapter 10, when he
comes to the realization that 'each one has a meaning of life to himself'
and that 'everybody has or ought to have a purpose apart from bearing
children ...' (p. 112). As far as Okolo is concerned, a human being cannot
live a full life without fulfilling that purpose. Okara is certainly grappling
with a very serious moral or ideological problem — the commitment of
the individual to a search for spiritual and moral values, and the
conviction that the individual has a role in bringing society to an
awareness of the need to search for these values. Because of his
commitment Okolo dies for his ideals. Modern capitalist society cannot
tolerate an individual who seeks to reform it and to turn it away from the
'shadow-devouring trinity of gold, iron, concrete' — three symbols of
decadent materialism.

However, the effectiveness of Okara's method in conveying this
message cannot be fully appreciated if the reader fails to see the parallels

between *The Voice* and the Bible. Okara employs the para-linguistic affective devices of symbolism and indirect reference to the Bible, and these become part of the total meaning of the novel. The powerful and opposing symbols of darkness and light which lend more colour to the poetic qualities of the novel have already been referred to. *The Voice* has close affinities with the Bible here. The light–darkness symbolism is a familiar feature of the Bible and is at the very centre of Christian belief. This is how St. John's Gospel opens:

> In the beginning was the Word, and the Word was with God, and the Word was God. He was in the beginning with God; all things were made through him, and without him was not anything made that was made. In him was life, and the life was the light of men. The light shines in the darkness, and the darkness has not overcome it.
>
> There was a man sent from God, whose name was John. He came for testimony, to bear witness to the light, that all might believe through him. He was not the light, but came to bear witness to the light.   (John 1: 1–8)

There are echoes of this and other passages in *The Voice*. Okolo and Tuere are constantly surrounded by darkness. Tuere is forever tending a flame of fire, and Okolo is forever searching for light. The darkness–light symbolism provides the author with a method of bringing into sharp contrast the struggle between Good and Evil in Okolo's society. The pervading darkness that envelopes Okolo and Tuere's world is the spiritual emptiness, the fanatical and selfish materialism in their society. By being associated with the light, Okolo and Tuere become like John the Baptist who came 'to bear witness to the light' — bringing truth to their corrupt and oppressive society.

But the affinity between *The Voice* and the Bible goes further than this. When Okolo and Ukale are tied back-to-back to a canoe, they leave their message taking root among the poorest of the masses. Tuere tells Ukule, the cripple: 'You stay in the town and in the days to come, tell our story and tend our spoken words.' To which Ukule replies: 'Your spoken words will not die.' (p. 172)

Tuere's words echo the last words of Jesus Christ to his apostles when he parted with them after his resurrection. In St. Mark's Gospel Jesus is reported as saying: 'Go into all the world and preach the gospel to the whole creation ...' (Mark 16: 14) and in St. Luke's Gospel: 'You are witnesses of these things. And behold, I send the promise of my Father upon you; but stay in the city, until you are clothed with power from on high.' (Luke 24: 48–9)

Obiechina sees a close relationship between Okolo the poet-reformer and Christ the Saviour who is condemned to suffering and crucifixion. This is certainly a valid interpretation, especially if we bear in mind the resemblances between the Bible and *The Voice* just discussed.[5] In addition Okolo's death resembles the death of Christ: not only did Christ die leaving a few men to spread his gospel, but he also died between two thieves, and Okolo is destined to die in the company of a woman who has been condemned by society as an outcast. But Okolo can be said to have a still more direct relationship with John the Baptist, described in the Bible as the voice of one 'crying in the wilderness'. The name Okolo means 'the voice' and the text itself testifies to this. 'I am the voice from the locked up insides which the Elders, not wanting the people to hear, want to stop me', says Okolo (p. 34). Thus Okara can be seen to be alluding obliquely to the Gospel stories of Jesus Christ and John the Baptist, both of whom preached a spiritual message which was unacceptable to the leaders of the Jewish people, a message that was revolutionary and disturbing to those who symbolized the values of the existing system.

The book definitely ends on an optimistic note. It is not possible to accept Palmer's categorical statement that 'the message of *The Voice* is pessimistic in the extreme'.[6] Although Okolo is condemned to death, the seed he has planted in the hearts of Tuere and Ukule will take root and begin to grow. The history of revolutions shows that many revolutionaries die before the advent of the change they fought for, or before the full consolidation of the revolution. Jesus died before Christianity became a movement, Lenin died soon after the Russian Revolution, Amilcar Cabral died before the independence of Guinea Bissau, so did Eduardo Mondlane of Mozambique. Okara does not leave us in the dark, like Awoonor who, at the end of his otherwise impressive novel, *This Earth My Brother*, has nothing tangible to offer us. Okara may be depressed by the political situation in Africa, but he gives us a sense of direction. If someone starts the ball rolling and tries to make the masses see the need for political and social change, his efforts will not be in vain. Ultimately victory is certain.

Conclusion

In *The Voice*, Okara uses the white man's language to show his rejection of the values of the white man. The experiment with Ijaw syntax, idioms and modes of thinking through the medium of English is a realistic assertion of the writer's cultural independence. To be independent, the African cannot throw overboard everything that he has received from his former colonial masters, but he can take what he has inherited and mould it in such a way as to serve his own purposes. This particularly applies to language. The African cannot immediately do away with the languages imposed upon him by colonialism, but he must use them so that they serve not the colonial master but himself; so that they reflect not the culture of the colonial master, but his own culture. Okara's method is to try as far as possible to utilize traditional African thought processes, traditional rhythms and traditional turns of phrase by employing the technique of transliteration.

But this is a method which has hazards as well as advantages. The use of African expressions brings an element of artificiality into the writer's style. The repetition of expressions like 'his inside', 'his shadow', 'no chest', and the collocation of certain words, for example, 'eyes' and 'right', 'head' and 'correct', as in the opening paragraphs of the book, does sound unnatural and some readers may be put off by this 'incorrect' English. It has been said of Tutuola that his style is not likely to be imitated and developed by other writers. The same can be said of Okara's style in *The Voice*. It is not a style that holds great promise for the future. African users of English are not likely to accept features of Okara's English in Standard African English.

Nevertheless there is no doubt that Okara's experiment will take its place as one of the most important in the history of Anglophone literature in Africa. Though the idiom sounds foreign to speakers of Standard English, Okara seldom sacrifices clarity, and readability is high. Transparency (semantic clarity) is an integral part of the book's simplicity. More than that the richness of imagery and symbolism that characterizes the book gives it a poetic quality that can only be paralleled by Armah's *Two Thousand Season*, if at all.

Through the complex interaction of atmosphere, symbolism and dramatic technique Okara creates passages of compelling power and passages which are memorable. This is particularly true of Chapter 5 where the evocative power of the language enables the reader to experience something of the fear and tension which Okolo undergoes, and thus compels him to read on to see what happens to Okolo. And putting aside the fact that Okara's Ijaw English at times sounds artificial, it can also be argued that the writer's language is conveniently *in character*. Izongo and other uneducated Africans use African modes of expression, while Abadi the man educated in the west, the product of western civilization who does not question the values of the west, is distinguished by his use of the white man's language, Standard English. Though educated, Okolo is fighting to assert the values of his people's ancestors, and so he speaks the ancestors' language except when talking to a white man. By associating his protagonist with the language and traditions of the people Okara resolves the conflict between theme and medium: a conflict which can arise in a novel seeking to assert African values in a foreign language.

Notes

1 See Palmer, *An Introduction to the African Novel* and Ravenscroft (1969) 'Introduction' to *The Voice* in Okara (1964).

2 Obiechina, 'Art and Artifice in Okara's *The Voice*', *Okike*, Vol. 1, No. 3.

3 See W. W. Skeat, *Langland's Vision of Piers Plowman*, pp. 1–50.

4 See 'African Speech — English Words', *Transition*, Vol. 3, No. 10.

5 See Obiechina, op. cit.

6 *An Introduction to the African Novel*, p. 158.

5 Chinua Achebe — *Arrow of God*

▼▼▼▼▼▼▼▼▼▼▼▼▼▼▼▼▼▼▼▼▼▼▼▼▼▼▼▼▼▼▼

Achebe on the English Language

In using a colonial language to express the African experience there is, as we have seen, a certain contradition. Chinua Achebe is explicit about this contridiction and the dilemma which it poses to the contemporary African writer. In his essay 'The African Writer and the English Language'[1] Achebe declares:

> The price a world language must be prepared to pay is submission to many different kinds of use. The African writer should aim to use English in a way that brings out his message best without altering the language to the extent that its value as a medium of international exchange will be lost. He should aim at fashioning out an English which is at once universal and able to carry his peculiar experience.   (p. 61)

Achebe's novel, *Arrow of God*, demonstrates his awareness of this dilemma from the very start. Here are the first two paragraphs:

> This was the third nightfall since he began to look for signs of the new moon. He knew it would come today but he always began his watch three days early because he must not take a risk. In this season of the year his task was not too difficult; he did not have to peer and search the sky as he might do when the rains came. Then the new moon sometimes hid itself for many days behind rain clouds so that when it finally came out it was already halfgrown. And while it played its game the Chief Priest sat up every evening waiting.
>
> His *obi* was built differently from other men's huts. There was the usual, long threshold in front but also a shorter one on the right as you entered. The eaves on this additional entrance were cut back so that sitting on the floor Ezeulu could watch that part of the sky where the moon had its door. It was getting darker and he constantly blinked to clear his eyes of the water that formed from gazing so intently.   (p. 1)

This passage gives us a good idea of the dialect which Achebe has chosen to write in — not pidgin English or a Nigerian dialect but

Standard English. We can however already see in this passage the influence of the writer's mother tongue. The word *obi*, for instance, is used untranslated from Igbo. Achebe writes in Standard English, but by no means in conventional English. He diverges into different directions depending on the interlocutor, the historical and social context, and on the interlocutor's age, sex, education and so on.

Language and Social Background

The social and historical context of *Arrow of God* is the time when European influence is beginning to have an impact on life in Eastern Nigeria, when missionaries and colonialists are closing in on Igbo society. Many parts of Nigeria and Igboland are already under the control of British colonial administrators and under the influence of missionaries, but Umuaro still lives according to its own traditional laws and religion. The interaction of traditional village Africans with colonial administrators, missionaries and semi-educated Africans is therefore inevitable. The conflicts that arise from the interaction of these various ethnic and social groups, is, as we shall see, the subject of Achebe's novel. In analysing the writer's use of language, therefore, we should take into account the fact that characters in the book have divergent linguistic, cultural and social backgrounds. Let us start by examining the language of one such group — the African.

The language of characters from traditional Igbo society

The Igbo society which Achebe depicts is highly organized and stratified. There is the Chief Priest, Ezeulu, the main character; there are the elders like Nwaka; there are groups of young men who work in age groups; and there are the women and children. Patterns of linguistic behaviour are attached to all these various groups. Here, for instance, is a passage depicting the speech of women and children:

> He beat his *ogene* GOME GOME GOME GOME ... and immediately children's voices took up the news on all sides. *Onwa atuo! ... onwa atuo! ... onwa atuo!* ... He put the stick back into the iron gong and leaned it on the wall.
>
> The little children in his compound joined the rest in welcoming the moon. Obiageli's tiny voice stood out like a small *ogene* among drums and flutes. He could also make out the voice of his youngest son, Nwafo. The women too were in the open, talking.
>
> 'Moon,' said the senior wife, Matefi, 'may your face meeting mine bring good fortune.'
>
> 'Where is it?' asked Ugoye, the younger wife. 'I don't see it. Or am I blind?'
>
> 'Don't you see beyond the top of the ukwa tree? Not there. Follow my finger.'
>
> 'Oho, I see it. Moon, may your face meeting mine bring good

fortune. But how is it sitting? I don't like its posture.'

'Why?' asked Matefi.

'I think it sits awkwardly — like an evil moon.'

'No,' said Matefi. 'A bad moon does not leave anyone in doubt. Like the one under which Okuata died. Its legs were up in the air.'

'Does the moon kill people?' asked Obiageli, tugging at her mother's cloth.

'What have I done to this child? Do you want to strip me naked?'

'I said does the moon kill people?'

'It kills little girls,' said Nwafo, her brother.

'I did not ask you, ant-hill nose.'

'You will soon cry, long throat.'

The moon kills little boys
The moon kills ant-hill nose
The moon kills little boys...' Obiageli turned everything into a song.   (pp. 2–3)

Achebe is obviously recording Igbo thought processes here. The sound of the *ogene* bell is heard through Igbo ears. It does not say 'ding-dong! ding-dong!' in the manner of English bells, but 'GOME GOME GOME GOME'. The capitalization of the onomatopoeic word 'GOME' and the italicization of other Igbo words have both a visual and an aesthetic appeal. It is as if the bell sounds louder when its sound is recorded in capitals! The excitement with which the new moon is heralded is evoked at the beginning of the passage, particularly in the Igbo words which, though untranslated, have an effect on the reader: '*onwa atuo! ... onwa atuo! ... onwa atuo! ...*' The superstitions of this traditional society, and the religious temperament of the women, come out in the invocation to the moon. As soon as the moon appears they are already thinking of the blessings or evil omen which it can bring. The kind of talk that is typical of children is also portrayed. Their language consists of questions, petty quarrels and songs.

Obiageli's music is commented on by the writer. Her idiolect is characterized by rhyming songs. But we know that songs and nursery rhymes are part of the day-to-day life of little children in a traditional African society, so Obiageli stands for a typical village girl of her age. The whole book reverberates with Obiageli's song and rhyme.

The passage I have quoted is given in its cultural context. It is not the speech of a particular woman or child, but portrays the type of language that is typical of women and children of such a society. We may contrast this passage with one where a young man, Edogo — Ezeulu's first son, the father of two children, one dead and the other alive — is thinking about his own father's actions:

A strange thought seized Edogo now. Could it be that their father had deliberately sent Oduche to the religion of the white man so as to disqualify him from the priesthood of Ulu? He put down the chisel with which he was absent-mindely straightening the intersecting lines on the iroko door. That would explain it! The priesthood would then fall on his youngest and favourite son. The reason which Ezeulu gave for his strange decision had never convinced anyone. If as he said he merely wanted one of his sons to be his eye and ear at this new assembly, why did he not send Nwafo who was close to his thoughts? No, that was not the reason. The priese wanted to have a hand in the choice of his successor. It was what anyone who knew Ezeulu would expect him to do. But was he not presuming too much? The choice of a priest lay with the deity. Was it likely that he would let the old priest force his hand. Although Edogo and Obika did not seem attracted to the office, that would not prevent the deity from choosing either of them or even Oduche, out of spite... (p. 92)

In this fine passage Achebe successfully conveys the seriousness of Edogo's thoughts. He is so absorbed in his thoughts that he lays down the instruments he has been using. The language is again Standard English, but it is interlarded with Igbo idioms, for instance, 'he merely wanted one of his sons to be his eye and ear', 'was it likely that he would let the old priest force his hand?' Edogo is a young but unwesternized Igbo man. His language is therefore different from the English of educated Nigerians like Obi Okonkwo in *No Longer at Ease*; at the same it is not like the language of Ezeulu or Nwaka. His language is quite plain, unmarked by the frequent use of proverbs. He is only a young man, not an elder, so his idiolect is not characterized by figurative expressions.

In traditional Igbo society the art of rhetoric is acquired by those who have accumulated the wisdom of the community through age and practice. This can be demonstrated by examining a passage where elders are discussing grave matters of state. In Chapter Two, for example, we meet the elders of Umuaro debating about sending an emissary to Okperi about a disputed piece of land. Ezeulu contends that the piece of farmland in question belongs to Okperi not to Umuaro. Nwaka disputes this — he stands up to speak:

'Umuaro kwenu!' Nwaka roared.
'Hem!' replied the men of Umuaro.
'Kwenu!'
'Hem!'
'Kweuzuenu!'
'Hem!'
He began to speak almost softly in the silence he had created with his salutation.

'Wisdom is like a goatskin bag; every man carries his own. Knowledge of the land is also like that. Ezeulu has told us what his father told him about the olden days. We know that a father does not speak falsely to his son. But we also know that the lore of the land is beyond the knowledge of many fathers. If Ezeulu had spoken about the great deity of Umuaro which he carries and which his fathers carried before him I would have paid attention to his voice. But he speaks about events which are older than Umuaro itself. I shall not be afraid to say that neither Ezeulu nor any other in his village can tell about these events.' There were murmurs of approval and disapproval but more of approval from the assembly of elders and men of title. Nwaka walked forward and back as he spoke; the eagle feather in his red cap and bronze band on his ankle marked him out as one of the lords of the land — a man favoured by Eru, the god of riches.

'My father told me a different story. He told me that Okperi people were wanderers. He told me three or four different places where they sojourned for a while and moved on again. They were driven away by Umuofia, then by Abame and Aninta. Would they go today and claim all those sites? Would they have laid claim on our farmland in the days before the white man turned us upside down? Elders and Ndichie of Umuaro, let everyone return to his house if we have no heart in the fight. We shall not be the first people who abandoned their farmland or even their homestead to avoid war. But let us not tell ourselves or our children that we did it because the land belonged to other people. Let us rather tell them that their fathers did not choose to fight. Let us tell them also that we marry the daughters of Okperi and their men marry out daughters, and that where there is this mingling men often lose the heart to fight. Umuaro Kwenu!'

'Hem!'

'Kwezuenu!'

'Hem!'

'I salute you all.'   (pp. 15–17)

The structure of this rhetorical speech is typical of speeches of this kind. There are six stages:

1. First of all there is a formal opening. The speaker greets the elders, who participate in the speech by returning the greeting.

2. After the formal opening the author either breaks in with a comment as in this case, or he lets the speaker go on to introduce the speech proper.

3. The speech itself frequently opens with a proverbial saying which serves as the basis of the speech and is then expanded. Thus Nwaka begins: 'Wisdom is like a goatskin bag; every man carries his own. Knowledge of the land is also like that ...'

4. At a suitable point in the speech, the author breaks in with a comment. He tells us about the mannerisms of the speaker and about the reactions of the audience to the speech.

5. Then comes the continuation of the speech when the orator drives his point home.

6. Finally, there is the conclusion: 'I salute you all'.

(In some speeches stage 2 and stage 4 do not feature, as in the case of Ezeulu's speech referred to below.)

Nwaka is undoubtedly an expert orator. This comes out particularly in the second part of the speech quoted above. He uses a number of devices which centre on the technique of repetition. In the first three sentences of the paragraph 'told me' recurs three times: 'My father told me ..., He told me that Okperi ..., He told me three or four ...' These sentences are both informational and affective. They give information to the listener; they also affect him, winning him to the speaker's point of view. Nwaka then reinforces the sentences with rhetorical questions: 'Would they go today ...?' 'Would they have laid ...?' The questions are meant to elicit the answer 'No' from the audience. The orator then goes on to throw a direct challenge at the elders, thereby dealing the final blow to Ezeulu's argument: 'Elders and Ndichie of Umuaro, let everyone return to his house if we have no heart in the fight ... But let us not tell ourselves ... Let us rather tell them ... Let us tell them ...' The repetition of 'let' and 'let us' surely has its desired effect of persuading the hearer.

The frequency of proverbs and illustrations in the speech of an elder seems to depend, at least in part, on the talents of the speaker. Though a great orator, Nwaka does not have as rich a storehouse of proverbial sayings as his enemy, Ezeulu. Ezeulu's talent in this regard becomes evident as soon as he opens his mouth to give a speech. Here is the first part of a speech he gives when emotions run high about the state of war between Umuaro and Okperi:

> *The reed we were blowing is now crushed.* When I spoke two markets ago in this very place I used the proverb of the she-goat. I was then talking to Ogbuefi Egonwanne who was the adult in the house. I told him that he should have spoken up against what we were planning, instead of which he *put a piece of live coal into a child's palm and asked him to carry it with care.* We have all seen with what care he carried it. I was not then talking to Egonwanne alone but to all the elders here who left what they should have done and did another, *who were in the house and yet the she-goat suffered in her parturition.'*   (p. 26, author's italics)

In this short paragraph there are as many as three proverbial sayings (italicized), and in the remaining part of the speech we get proverb after proverb in addition to an illustrative story.

In some of his narrative passages, Achebe attempts to capture both the structure of the original language and the world view of its speakers. Here, for example, is the author relating how the war was fought between Umuaro and Okperi:

> The war was waged from one Afo to the next. On the day it began Umuaro killed two men of Okperi. The next day was Nkwo, and so there was no fighting. On the two following days, Eke and Oye, the fighting grew fierce. Umuaro killed four men and Okperi replied

with three, one of the three being Akukalia's brother, Okoye. The next day, Afo, saw the war brought to a sudden close. The white man, Wintabota, brought soldiers to Umuaro and stopped it. The story of what these soldiers did in Abame was still told with fear, and so Umuaro made no effort to resist but laid down their arms. Although they were not yet satisfied they could say without shame that Akukalia's death had been avenged, that they had provided him with three men on whom to rest his head. It was also a good thing perhaps that the war was stopped. The death of Akukalia and his brother in one and the same dispute showed that Ekwensu's hand was in it.

The white man, not satisfied that he had stopped the war, had gathered all the guns in Umuaro and asked the soldiers to break them in the face of all, except three or four which he carried away. Afterwards he sat in judgement over Umuaro and Okperi and give the disputed land to Okperi.   (p. 28)

The time concepts of the Igbo people are reflected here. The Igbo concept of the week comes out in the use of the words 'Afo', 'Nkwo', 'Eke', 'Oye'. It would seem that the traditional Igbo week was four days long, and if that is the case the war lasted a whole week although on the second day of the week, Nkwo, there was no fighting. The white man intervened when the war had entered its second week. The passage also reveals something about the Igbo people's system of beliefs. The fact that two brothers, Akukalia and his brother, died in the same war, is sufficient to show that there was something wrong in the way the war was conducted. 'It showed that 'Ekwensu's hand was in it'. If this means Umuaro was being punished by the gods, it is one proof that the Chief Priest was right when he used a proverb to explain that Ulu would not fight in aid of those whose cause was not just: 'If you go to war to avenge a man who passed shit on the head of his mother's father, Ulu will not follow you to be soiled in the corruption' (p. 27).

Throughout this novel the use of proverbs in the African passages is, of course, very significant. Achebe's use of proverbs has already been explored by other writers and will be discussed in greater detail in a later section.[2] But in the present context it should be emphasized that Achebe does not throw proverbs about indiscriminately or as the whim takes him. Obiechina has said: 'Proverbs are the kernels which contain the wisdom of the traditional people. They are philosophical and moral expositions shrunk to a few words...'[3] It follows that those in society who have acquired the wisdom of their forefathers, those who are the upholders of the beliefs and philosophy of the community, are the people who are likely to make frequent use of proverbs. It is proper therefore that in *Arrow of God* Ezeulu, the Chief Priest of the people and the very pillar and corner-stone of the people's culture and customs, should appear to be the most gifted user of proverbs. Throughout *Arrow of God* it is in those chapters and passages which depict the traditional African that Igbo modes of expression are used.

The language of Englishmen

Achebe's handling of the language of English people may be studied in Chapters Three and Five, where the writer deals mainly with Captain Winterbottom and Mr Clarke.

One interesting feature of Chapter Three, in contrast with chapters which depict the African way of life, is the recurrence of terms referring to rank and title in the British colonial administration. Thus on p. 31 we meet the following: 'Administration', 'Assistant Superintendent', 'Public Works Department', 'Captain Winterbottom', 'District Officer'. These are terms which do not appear in those parts of the book which reflect African life and traditional social structures.

Captain Winterbottom has lent Tony Clarke a book by George Allen, *The Pacification of the Primitive Tribes of the Lower Niger*. Achebe has devised a title and extract which are a caricature of the British attitude to imperialism and to the indigenous people in the colonies. The last chapter headed The Call displays the enthusiasm and missionary zeal of an administrator in the British Civil Service:

> For those seeking but a comfortable living and a quiet occupation Nigeria is closed and will be closed until the earth has lost some of its deadly fertility and until the people live under something like sanitary conditions. But for those in search of a strenuous life, for those who can deal with men as others deal with material, who can grasp situations, coax events, shape destinies and ride on the crest of a wave of time Nigeria is holding out her hands. For men who in India have made the Briton the law-maker, the organizer, the engineer of the world, this new, old land has great rewards and honourable work. I know we can find the men. Our mothers do not draw us with nervous grip back to the fireside of boyhood, back into the home circle, back to the purposeless sports of middle life; it is our greatest pride that they do — albeit tearfully — send us fearless and erect, to lead the backward races into line. "Surely we are the people!" Shall it be the Little Englander for whom the Norman fought the Saxon on his field? Was it for him the archers bled at Crécy and Poitiers, or Cromwell drilled his men? Is it only for the desk our youngsters read of Drake and Frobisher, of Nelson, Clive and men like Mungo Park? Is it for the counting-house they learn of Carthage, Greece and Rome? No, no; a thousand times no! The British race will take its place, the British blood will tell. Son after son will leave the Mersey, strong in the will of his parents today, stronger in the deed of his fathers in the past, braving the climate, taking the risks, playing his best in the game of life.' (p. 33)

After reading this passage Mr Clarke says 'That's rather good', and it indeed expresses the classical colonial viewpoint, in the Queen's English. Here is a man who believes that British colonialism is a noble mission which must be fulfilled for the betterment of mankind. The enthusiasm of the writer is evident in the rhetorical questions, the jubilant exclamations, in the powerful movement and rhythm of the language, as well as in the excited references to the proud history and great heroes of Great Britain. The reference to Carthage, Greece and Rome is a clear indication of George Allen's belief that Britain is as great in the modern world as those three nations were in the ancient world. The British race is portrayed as a race of great heroes to whom the world owes the meaning of civilization. At the same time the British image of colonial subjects is projected. This comes out in the very title of the book, with the derogatory connotations of the words 'Primitive Tribes'. George Allen's image of the African coincides with that of Captain Winterbottom, as we shall see.

Achebe portrays Captain Winterbottom as a typical colonial in terms of his mentality and attitudes. He is probably not a very good specimen of an Englishman, but his mind is thoroughly English. In the following passage we hear him and Mr Clarke carrying out a conversation that is typical of Englishmen — a conversation about the weather:

> 'It's nice and cool today, thank God.'
> 'Yes, the first rain was pretty much overdue,' said Captain Winterbottom.
> 'I had no idea what a tropical storm looked like. It will be cooler now, I suppose.'
> 'Well, not exactly. It will be fairly cool for a couple of days, that's all. You see, the rainy season doesn't really begin until May or even June. Do sit down. Did you enjoy that?'   (pp. 34–5)

The idiom is thoroughly English. In this and other passages something of Winterbottom's turn of mind is indicated. He is portrayed as one who boasts about and exaggerates his knowledge of Nigeria, the 'natives' and colonial administration. That he exaggerates his knowledge of the 'natives' is shown in passages where he talks glibly and 'expertly' about them, while misinterpreting their culture. On page 58, for example, *obi* is translated as 'King', but we know from the context of the first page in the book that *obi* refers to a house. (In the glossary at the end of *Things Fall Apart* it is translated as 'the large living quarters of the head of the family'.)

Captain Winterbottom's attitude to both Africans and British colonial officers is interesting. It is made clear in the following passage where he is talking to Tony Clarke:

> 'I see you are one of the progressive ones. When you've been here as long as Allen was and understood the native a little more you

might begin to see things in a slightly different light. If you saw, as I did, a man buried alive up to his neck with a piece of roast yam on his head to attract vultures you know... Well, never mind. We British are a curious bunch, doing everything half-heartedly. Look at the French. They are not ashamed to teach their culture to backward races under their charge. Their attitude to the native ruler is clear. They say to him: "This land has belonged to you because you have been strong enough to hold it. By the same token it now belongs to us. If you are not satisfied come out and fight us." What do we British do? We flounder from one expedient to its opposite. We do not only promise to secure old savage tyrants on their thrones — or more likely filthy animal skins — we not only do that, but we now go out of our way to invent chiefs where there were none before. They make me sick.' He swallowed what was left in his glass and shouted to Boniface for another glass. 'I wouldn't really mind if this dithering was left to old fossils in Lagos, but when young Political Officers get infected I just give up. If someone is positive we call him smug.' (p. 36)

To Winterbottom the African is a savage 'native' with whom there should be no compromise. He simply must submit to British rule or face the might of the British empire. The word 'native' falls readily from Winterbottom's lips. African rulers are 'savage tyrants'; their thrones are 'filthy animal skins'. In another passage (p. 38) we are told that Africans easily perjure themselves and are 'great liars'. But Captain Winterbottom does not hide his attitude to British officers either. He has no respect for those who compromise with natives, and is impatient with liberal young political officers whom he sarcastically calls 'the progressive ones'. As for the senior political officers who are fond of 'dithering' in their dealings with natives, Captain Winterbottom finds it appropriate to call them 'old fossils'. The little respect the Captain has for his African servant shows itself in his constant shouts at him: 'Boniface!'

In Chapters Three and Five Achebe achieves various kinds of effect through the use of language. He portrays the British man's attitude towards Africans largely through the former's tenor of discourse. Captain Winterbottom's idiom and his use of such words as 'native', 'savage', 'backward race', together help in creating the white man's image of the black man. These terms are not used by the Africans themselves. So Achebe shows that they are inventions of the white man's mind and represent not objective truth, but the white man's subjective image of the African. In these two chapters we therefore see the Igbo society through the eyes and mind of the white man. Thus an Igbo man's religious symbol is described as a 'fetish' (p. 37), while Captain Winterbottom's man servant is called a 'Small Boy' (p. 35). Africans would never refer to themselves and their religious things in those terms. The idea which the

word *Ikenga* calls up in an Igbo mind is very different from the sense
conveyed by the English term for the same thing, 'fetish'.

The picture of Captain Winterbottom that we are given in these and
other chapters is that of an unpleasant and embittered man. He is bitter
for two reasons: first, another man walked away with his wife in his
absence (and thus, presumably, humiliated him); and secondly, he has
been in the colonial service for a long time but has not been promoted
above the rank of District Officer (p. 58). At times his bitterness comes
out in the bluntness and rudeness of his language. Here is his reaction to
the Lieutenant-Governor's memorandum:

> Words, words, words. Civilization, African mind, African
> atmosphere. Has His Honour ever rescued a man buried alive up
> to his neck, with a piece of roast yam on his head to attract
> vultures? He began to pace up and down again. But why couldn't
> someone tell the bloody man that the whole damn thing was stupid
> and futile. He knew why. They were all afraid of losing their
> promotion or the O.B.E.   (p. 56)

The contempt in the speaker's voice is clear; but what is more
interesting is his use of expressions like 'the bloody man', 'the whole
damn thing', 'stupid and futile' which one might not associate with the
dignified Captain. This kind of language also appears near the beginning
of the chapter where the Captain is deriding a man who was once his
junior but is now his senior, having been promoted over him. 'Any fool
can be promoted,' says Captain Winterbottom, 'provided he does
nothing but try' (p. 54–5).

Mr Clarke and Captain Winterbottom illustrate Achebe's amazing
ability to create memorable characters outside his or our range of
sympathy and identification. This he does largely by the idiolect he
constructs for their speech.

The language of semi-literate Africans

Apart from the traditional African community and the English-speaking
community another linguistic group in Eastern Nigeria was springing up
at the time when the events of the novel occurred — that of the urbanized
and semi-literate African. This group was composed mainly of
employees of the colonial administration and personal servants of
colonial officers — people such as Captain Winterbottom's 'small boy'.
The policemen who are sent to arrest Ezeulu are in this group. When
speaking to their social equals or to white people they use pidgin English,
but they also know the languages of their respective home backgrounds.
Their linguistic behaviour is demonstrated by the following passage:

> Meanwhile the policemen arrived at Ezeulu's hut. They were then
> no longer in the mood for playing. They spoke sharply, baring all
> their weapons at once.

'Which one of you is called Ezeulu?' asked the corporal.

'Which Ezeulu?' asked Edogo.

'Don't ask me which Ezeulu again or I shall slap okro seeds out of your mouth. I say who is called Ezeulu here?'

'And I say which Ezeulu? Or don't you know who you are looking for?' The four men in the hut said nothing. Women and children thronged the door leading from the hut into the inner compound. There was fear and anxiety in the faces.

'All right,' said the corporal in English. 'Jus now you go sabby which Ezeulu. Gi me dat ting.' This last sentence was directed to his companion who immediately produced the handcuffs from his pocket...

The two policemen conferred in the white man's tongue to the great admiration of the villagers.

'Sometime na dat two porson we cross for road,' said the corporal.

'Sometime na dem,' said his companion. 'But we no go return back jus like dat. All dis waka wey we waka come here no fit go for nating.'

The corporal thought about it. The other continued:

'Sometime na lie dem de lie. I no wan make dem put trouble for we head.'

The corporal still thought about it. He was convinced that the men spoke the truth but it was necessary to frighten them a little, if only to coax a sizeable 'kola' out of them. He addressed them in Ibo:

'We think that you may be telling us a lie and so we must make quite sure otherwise the white man will punish us. What we shall do then is to take two of you — handcuffed — to Okperi. If we find Ezeulu there we shall set you free; if not ...' He completed with a sideways movement of the head which spoke more clearly than words. Which two shall we take?'   (pp. 152–4)

The arrogance of their opening words is clear. They are using the people's language here, not the white man's language, but they don't speak in the way the people speak. They have observed and heard the white man speak to Africans in this manner, and they are doing likewise. They speak with arrogance in the knowledge that they represent the white man's power and authority, and they have the white man's weapons to prove that authority to anybody who would dare challenge it. When they speak to one another they use pidgin, but when they address the people they speak in Igbo. In the process of this alternation from one language to another, the listener is left in no doubt that the speaker is proud of what he considers to be the white man's language.

The facility to change from the local language to pidgin is not always the result of pomp or linguistic chauvinism. As pidgin is a lingua franca, the code-switching will sometimes be determined by the linguistic backgrounds of the interlocutors involved. Thus Captain Winterbottom's 'small boy' speaks to his boss in pidgin English, not Igbo. (It is usually the case that the white man does not waste his time learning the language of his subjects or servants and expects them to speak English.) In the same way when a semi-literate African speaks to a fellow African, but one who does not share the same linguistic background, he may switch over to the white man's language, be it English proper or pidgin. Thus John Nwodika uses pidgin for the benefit of a non-Igbo speaking African:

> 'Did I not say so?' he asked the other servants after their master had been removed to hospital. 'Was it for nothing I refused to follow the policemen? I told them that the Chief Priest of Umuaro is not a soup you can lick in a hurry.' His voice carried a note of pride. 'Our master thinks that because he is a white man our medicine cannot touch him.' He switched over to English for the benefit of Clarke's steward who came in just then and who did not speak Ibo.
>
> 'I use to tellam say blackman juju no be someting wey man fit take play. But when I tellam na so so laugh im de laugh. When he finish laugh he call me John and I say Massa. He say You talk bush talk. I tellam say O-o, one day go be one day. You no see now?'   (p. 155)

Achebe uses pidgin English much more frequently in those novels whose setting is in more modern times, for example, *No Longer at Ease* and *A Man of the People*.

Culture Contact and Language

Achebe employs several methods to portray culture contact and culture conflict in *Arrow of God*. Chief among these in terms of stylistic criticism are: clashes in patterns of linguistic behaviour, para-linguistic affective devices, and proverbs.

Clashes in patterns of linguistic behaviour

Pidgin is the result of language contact. West African pidgin is a mixture of English and the local languages. Now the main theme of *Arrow of God* can be summarized as that of culture contact and culture conflict in a situation where a culture which was previously self-sufficient begins to disintegrate in the face of an onslaught from the culture of an alien people who are politically more powerful. The contradictions in Ezeulu's society are of course multifarious, as we shall see in the last section of the chapter. But the greatest contradiction is the one between the culture of Umuaro and the culture of the new arrivals — the British Administration and the missionaries. The contradictions between

Ezeulu and the people of Umuaro only serve to precipitate the weakening of the local culture and the victory of the new imperialist culture.

Now culture contact in colonial countries had an important impact on languages, and on patterns of linguistic behaviour and etiquette. To Ezeulu and the people of Umuaro the sudden change in the patterns of linguistic behaviour comes as a shock, and is partly responsible for the hostile attitude which Ezeulu adopts towards his friend Winterbottom. At the same time Nwaka takes the opportunity to isolate the Chief Priest from the people of Umuaro by hammering the point that, since Ezeulu has been friends with the white man, there is nothing wrong in the way Winterbottom has treated him (p. 143 ff). The point is that the Chief Priest is not puzzled by the fact that he is summoned by Winterbottom, but he is annoyed and indeed astonished and stunned by the way in which the message is delivered, especially as it is delivered by people who are fully conversant with the norms of conduct and patterns of linguistic behaviour among the people of Umuaro. Here is the way Achebe represents the clash:

> The Court Messenger removed his blue fez and planted it on his knee exposing a clean-shaven head shining with sweat. The edge of the cap left a ring round the head. He cleared his throat and spoke, almost for the first time.
>
> 'I salute you all.' He brought out a very small book from his breast pocket and opened it in the manner of a white man.
>
> 'Which one of you is called Ezeulu?' he asked from the book and then looked up and around the hut.
>
> No one spoke; they were all too astonished. Akuebue was the first to recover.
>
> 'Look round and count your teeth with your tongue,' he said. 'Sit down, Obika, you must expect foreigners to talk through the nose.'
>
> 'You say you are a man of Umuru?' asked Ezeulu. 'Do you have priests and elders there?'
>
> 'Do not take my question amiss. The white man has his own way of doing things. Before he does anything to you he will first ask you your name and the answer must come from your own lips.'
>
> 'If you have any grain of sense in your belly,' said Obika, 'you will know that you are not in the house of the white man but in Umuaro in the house of the Chief Priest of Ulu.' (pp. 137–8)

In the following passage the nature of the message to Ezeulu is explained, and the difference between the white man's way of doing things and the black man's ways is further clarified:

> The Court Messenger continued to smile menacingly. 'Yes,' he said. 'Your friend Wintabota' (he mouthed the name in the

ignorant fashion of his hearers) 'has ordered you to appear before
him tomorrow morning.'

'Where?' asked Edogo.
'Where else but in his office in Okperi.'
'The fellow is mad,' said Obika.
'No, my friend. If anyone is mad it's you. Anyhow, Ezeulu must
prepare at once. Fortunately the new road makes even a cripple
hungry for a walk. We set out this morning at the first cock-crow
and before we knew where we were we had got here.'
'I said the fellow is mad. Who ...'
'He is not mad,' said Ezeulu.
'He is a messenger and he must give the message as it was given
him. Let him finish.'
'I have finished,' said the other. 'But I ask whoever owns this young
man to advise him for his own good.'
'You are sure you have given all the message?'
'Yes, the white man is not like black men. He does not waste his
words.'   (p. 138–9)

In this conversation, the relationships between the participants are not
observed. In a traditional society like the Umuaro community, the
young must adopt a proper attitude and an appropriate tone of voice
when speaking to elders; but here, even the Chief Priest of Ulu is not
respected. This has dire consequences. The most immediate effect is that
Obika explodes openly and Ezeulu boils inwardly without showing his
feelings to the white man's messenger.

Para-linguistic affective devices

Achebe uses a number of para-linguistic affective devices to portray
culture conflict and the disintegration of Igbo culture. The python, for
example, features as a symbol of the traditional religion and the bell as a
symbol of the new. These two are seen in contrast with one another.
Before Oduche's attempt to suffocate the python is discovered, Ezeulu
hears the bell (p. 42). Mr Goodcountry, the new Christian teacher,
regards the python as the very symbol and corner-stone of the
traditional religion and regards it as every Christian's bounden duty to
kill it (p. 47). But Moses Unachukwu does not take this extreme view of
Christian doctrine, for he tells Mr Goodcountry that 'neither the Bible
nor the catechism asked converts to kill the python' (p. 48). Seen from the
point of view of Moses Unachukwu's interpretation of Christian
theology, the python and the bell are non-antagonistic contradictions
which can be reconciled; but if Mr Goodcountry's interpretation is taken
as the norm, then the bell and the python symbolize two antagonistic
contradictions which can only be resolved by the victory of the one and
the vanquishing of the other. Oduche and the likes of him are converted

to Mr Goodcountry's standpoint. In support of Mr Goodcountry Oduche says: 'It is not true that the Bible does not ask us to kill the serpent. Did not God tell Adam to crush its head after it had deceived his wife?' (p. 49).

Unachukwu is a local Christian who wants to see Christianity in the context of his own culture; Goodcountry represents the missionary point of view which regards all aspects of the traditional religion as contrary to the Word of God. Those like Oduche who go to the missionary school will automatically accept the missionary point of view.

Achebe also employs another para-linguistic affective device — the dream motif. The dream is used several times in the book as a device for foreshadowing subsequent events, as a means of prophesying for the dreamer the way things are going to turn out. On his first night in Okperi, for instance, Ezeulu dreams a strange dream where he sees the elders of Umuaro, Nwaka among them, at loggerheads with the Chief Priest of Ulu. He sees them refusing to obey the Chief Priest, some even spitting on his face and calling him 'the priest of a dead god' (p. 159). The dream is so violent that Ezeulu actually shouts in his sleep, and Obika hears him saying something which shows the nature of the struggle between the two contending religions — the fact that they cannot coexist in the same culture, the one must drive out the other: 'You were quarrelling with someone and saying you would see who would drive the other away' (p. 159).

The most haunting dream occurs towards the end of the book, when the struggle between the various opposing forces has reached its peak, when the reader is now fully involved in the events of the story. Here it is necessary to quote a fairly long extract, for this is an important passage where Achebe brings together several para-linguistic affective devices for maximum effect. The bell and the python are seen in conflict with each other, and this happens in the context of a dream where other symbolic devices are used:

> In the night Ezeulu dreamt one of those strange dreams which were more than ordinary dreams. When he woke up everything stood out with the detail and clarity of daylight, like the one he had dreamt in Okperi.
>
> He was sitting in his *obi*. From the sound of the voices the mourners seemed to be passing behind his compound, beyond the tall, red walls. This worried him a good deal because there was no path there. Who were these people then who made a path behind his compound? He told himself that he must go out and challenge them because it was said that unless a man wrestled with those who walked behind his compound the path never closed. But he lacked resolution and stood where he was. Meanwhile the voices and the drums and flutes grew louder. They sang the song with which a man was carried to the bush for burial:

>   Look! a python
>   Look! a python
>   Yes, it lies across the way.

As usual the song came in different waves like gusts of storm
following on each other's heels. The mourners in front sang a little
ahead of those in the middle near the corpse and these were again
ahead of those at the rear. The drums came with this last wave.

Ezeulu raised his voice to summon his family to join him in
challenging the trespassers but his compound was deserted. His
irresolution turned into alarm. He ran into Matefi's hut but all he
saw were the ashes of a long-dead fire. He rushed out and ran into
Ugoye's hut calling her and her children but her hut was already
falling in and a few blades of grass had sprouted on the thatch. He
was running towards Obika's hut when a new voice behind the
compound brought him to a sudden halt. The noise of the burial
party had since disappeared in the distance. But beside the sorrow
of the solitary voice that now wailed after them they might have
been returning with a bride. The sweet agony of the solitary singer
settled like dew on the head.

>   I was born when lizards were in ones and twos
>   A child of Idemili. The difficult tear-drops
>   Of Sky's first weeping drew my spots. Being
>   Sky-born I walked the earth with royal gait
>   And mourners saw me coiled across their path.
>   But of late
>   A strange bell
>   Has been ringing a song of desolation:
>   Leave your yams and cocoyams
>   And come to school.
>   And I must scuttle away in haste
>   When children in play or in earnest cry:
>   Look! a Christian is on the way.
>   Ha ha ha ha ha ha ha ha ha ha ha ha ha... (pp. 221–2)

This is a very powerful passage. The reader is struck by and shares the
weird atmosphere in which Ezeulu finds himself in the dream. The
strangeness of the darkness of the night is effectively conveyed. The
passage is vivid and dramatic. The dramatic element comes out in the
part where Ezeulu is portrayed as running to and fro in alarm. As he runs
into Matefi's hut, he finds only 'the ashes of a long-dead fire'; Ugoye's hut
is already 'falling in'. These are signs of death; they are signs of the
disintegration, not only of his own home, but of all that he stands for —
his religion, his way of life, his culture. He sees these signs against the
background of mourning voices. The mourning may have a significance
wider than the affairs of his own family, but there is no doubt that it
points to something much more immediate than the death of his society's

culture; the mourners are mourning his son Obika, who has died performing a ritual.

The fact that the dream portends not only Obika's death, not only the destruction of Ezeulu's home, but also the disintegration of all that he, as Chief Priest, stands for — the whole cultural fabric of his society — is symbolized by the song of the python which the Chief Priest hears as 'the sweet agony of the solitary singer'. The sad song embodies both the legendary history of the sacred python, and the combat between the python and the bell, leading to the vanquishing of the former. If in his Okperi dream Ezeulu pronounced the statement: 'We will see who will drive the other way', here is the answer: the python 'must scuttle away in haste'.

Proverbs

We have already pointed out the significance of proverbs in *Arrow of God* as in Igbo society. Throughout the book proverbs are used by various characters in public speeches, in conversation, in rituals and in reflective moments when characters like Ezeulu are engaged in active thinking. The proverb is consequently one of the major stylistic features of the book and is used by the author to give unity and depth of meaning to his narrative. It is proper therefore that, in portraying the disintegration of Igbo culture, the writer should exploit this device so as to point his moral and to give us an insight into the nature of the contradictions which he exposes through the artistic medium of the novel. The sphere of reference of some of these proverbs extends beyond the immediate context in which they are uttered by the speaker, to encompass significances far wider than the speaker himself is aware of. Shakespeare uses dramatic irony in such a way that the reader sees more in what a character says than the character does at the moment of speaking. In the same way the reader who has followed Achebe's narrative, and the interaction of plot and character, is able to view the moral of the novel as a complex whole; he is in a position to see the consequences of what the various characters have said and done. He is able to see more meaning in at least some of the proverbs than the characters themselves. For a sensitive reader the proverbs are part of the message which the entire novel attempts to give. This comes out very clearly in the last chapter where the ritual called *ogbazulobodo* is performed. Obika is asked by the son of the dead man to be the spirit *ogbazulobodo*, a spirit who runs 'leaving *potent words* in the air behind' (p. 225). And for almost two pages we hear proverb after proverb falling from the spirit's lips. That this service is performed at this point in the novel is important not only in view of the death of Obika which is the climax of the event, but also because in order to bring unity and coherence to his narrative Achebe must at this point sum up the events of the book by referring indirectly, proverbially, to the consequences of some of the actions we have witnessed. I will give examples of how the proverbs used in this part of the book can be related to what has gone on in the novel. In the examples given below *P* stands for 'proverb' and *I* for 'interpretation':

P   The fly that struts on a mound of excrement wastes his time; the mound will always be greater than the fly (p. 225).
I   Ezeulu and the people of Umuaro might try to resist the pressures closing in on them in the form of a new religion and a foreign political administration, but these external forces are so powerful that the Umuaro people's resistance is bound to be ineffectual.
P   The fly that has no one to advise him follows the corpse into the ground (p. 226).
I   Ezeulu refuses to take other people's advice on the question of sending his son to the Christian Church, and the son turns out to be instrumental in the destruction of the traditional religion of which Ezeulu is the symbol. In Ezeulu's own words, Oduche becomes 'lizard that ruined his own mother's funeral' (p. 221). Ezeulu's strongheadedness in this and other matters leads to his own destruction.
P   The mighty tree falls and the little birds scatter in the bush (p. 226).
I   When Ezeulu, the Chief Priest of Ulu and the pillar of the culture and religion of Umuaro is destroyed, his people are also destroyed with him.
P   The very Thing which kills Mother Rat is always there to make sure that its young ones never open their eyes (p. 226).
I   When the Chief Priest of Ulu is paving the road to his doom by his own actions, the people of Umuaro, Nwaka's followers in particular, are at the same time blind to the fact that his destruction is their own destruction and that in pitting themselves against the Chief Priest they are participating in the disintegration of the whole fabric of their social system.
P   When death wants to take a little dog it prevents it from smelling even excrement (p. 226).
I   The dynamics of the situation prevent Ezeulu from realizing that his own actions (in punishing the people of Umuaro) can only lead to his own destruction and that of his family.

My interpretation of these proverbs as symbols used to represent the disintegration of Igbo culture is borne out by the fact that they are said in the context of a funeral ritual and a ritual which is immediately followed by the death of the utterer of these sayings. In other words, during the ritual Obika embodies the Igbo culture and his words are the expression of that culture. His death is thus symbolic of the death of the whole culture. In a very subtle manner Achebe has successfully enacted the death of his forefathers' culture by making use of its own rituals and its own modes of expression through the medium of a foreign language.

For Ezeulu, Obika's death is the final blow. He realizes that his son's death has a significance wider than itself: 'What could it point to but the collapse and ruin of all things' (p. 229). The death of his son sends him mad, and when Umuaro is deprived of its High Priest, the British Administration and the Christian Church triumph in the person of Captain Winterbottom and Mr Goodcountry.

Aesthetic Qualities

I would like to close the chapter by making a short review of the aesthetic qualities of *Arrow of God*.

First, it is important to emphasize that any account of such qualities in *Arrow of God* should include a discussion of Achebe's use of language. The role that language plays in deepening our understanding of the author's theme, in portraying character, and in showing the social rank and background of the speaker has been referred to. With regard to character we have noted how the personality of Winterbottom presents itself through the use of language. Ezeulu, the main character, is memorable partly from what he does, but largely from the language he uses. It has already been pointed out that as Chief Priest and one of the elders of Umuaro, he has acquired knowledge of the community's cultural heritage, including the art of speaking which is highly prized in the society — hence his expert use of proverbs. Ezeulu is also a forceful and mysterious character, being partly human and partly spirit. The fecundity of his mind, and the mystery that surrounds him, are fully realized through the powers of speech with which the author has invested him.

We begin to have a true picture of Ezeulu in Chapter Twelve where we meet him engaged in a very serious discussion with Akeubue, the grand old man who is Ezeulu's good friend in good weather and in bad. One of the issues they touch upon is that of the arrival of the white man. Ezeulu argues that if the Igbos want to drive the white man away successfully they should not attempt to do it immediately, but should wait until he is 'tired of his visit'. His argument shows how sharp-minded he is: at this time he can already foresee that in order to defeat the white man the African must first of all learn the former's ways. That is partly why he sends his son to the Christian Church to be educated. In an amazing act of prophecy, he had said to his son: 'my spirit tells me that those who do not befriend the white man today will be saying *had we known* tomorrow' (p. 46). We realize from this that although he precipitates his own destruction by sending his son to the Christian Church, Ezeulu's decision is defensible because in the long run it is the mission-educated African who is going to have sufficient resources to cope with the white man. However, the power of his words is what concerns us here, the forceful character that emerges from his use of language:

> If we now want him to go away again we must either wait until he is
> tired of his visit or we must drive him away. Do you think you can

drive him away by blaming Ezeulu? You may try, and the day I
hear that you have succeeded I shall come and shake your hand. I
have my own way and I shall follow it. I can see things where other
men are blind. That is why I am Known and at the same time I am
Unknowable. You are my friend and you know whether I am a
thief or a murderer or an honest man. But you cannot know the
Thing which beats the drum to which Ezeulu dances. I can see
tomorrow; that is why I can tell Umuaro: *come out from this
because there is death there* or *do this because there is profit in it.* If
they listen to me, o-o; if they refuse to listen, o-o. I have passed the
stage of dancing to receive presents.   (p. 132)

Defending himself for sending his son to a strange religion, he has this
to say:

'Shall I tell you why I sent my son? Then listen. A disease that has
never been seen before cannot be cured with everyday herbs. When
we want to make a charm we look for the animal whose blood can
match its power; if a chicken cannot do it we look for a goat or a
ram; if that is not sufficient we send for a bull. But sometimes even a
bull does not suffice, then we must look for a human. Do you think
it is the sound of the death-cry gurgling through blood that we
want to hear? No, my friend, we do it because we have reached the
very end of things and we know that neither a cock nor a goat nor
even a bull will do. And our fathers have told us that it may even
happen to an unfortunate generation that they are pushed beyond
the end of things, and their back is broken and hung over a fire.
When this happens they may sacrifice their own blood. This is
what our sages meant when they said that a man who has nowhere
else to put his hand for support puts it on his own knee. That was
why our ancestors when they were pushed beyond the end of things
by the warriors of Abam sacrificed not a stranger but one of
themselves and made the great medicine which they called
Ulu.'   (pp. 133–4)

These are among the most magnificent passages of the whole novel, in
which Achebe strikes at his highest level of abstraction yet. In the second
passage especially Ezeulu expresses deep thoughts in concrete images.
The metaphors refer to animals, medicines, human suffering and
sacrifice. The abstraction we get in these passages is a result of intense
feeling, philosophical concentration, and an attempt to reach into the
very essence of things. The intensity of feeling is evident in such phrases
as 'the sound of the death-cry gurgling through blood', 'we have reached
the end of things', 'their back is broken and hung over a fire'. This is prose
elevated to poetry of the highest order. It is in this chapter and in these
passages that we are first moved to pity; it is in these passages that we
really begin to identify with this mysterious man with whom we have
little in common; it is here that we begin to feel the compelling power of

the novel. That in these passages Achebe has, through Ezeulu risen to great heights, is clear from p. 135: 'For a long time they ate in silence and when they began to talk again it was about less weighty things'.

Chapter Twelve is a major turning point in the book. Unlike *Things Fall Apart*, *Arrow of God* is not a book that fascinates and engages the reader as soon as he picks it up to read. The reasons for this are varied. We may start by considering the audience. The narrator is the author himself who tells the story in the third person, giving himself the privilege of entering his characters' minds and recording their innermost thoughts. The narrator is addressing both an African and a western English-speaking audience. He is very successful in his use of African idioms in an English novel — non-Igbo speakers are able to follow the story and to understand the Igbo proverbs and expressions used in the novel. There are, however, some minor shortcomings in the language. Achebe uses many Igbo terms such as *chi*, *obi*, *ogene*. These are not translated and the reader is expected to understand them in the context in which they are used. In some instances, however, these untranslated terms are somewhat obscure, the reader can only have a vague idea of what they stand for, and this tends to slow down his reading speed as he attempts to puzzle out what they mean. (*In Things Fall Apart* Achebe found it necessary to attach a glossary of Igbo words and phrases to the novel.) *Arrow of God* is also too culture-bound and sociologically oriented. The emphasis on the multifarious aspects of Igbo society tends to distract the reader and to hamper the smooth flow of events. Young non-Igbo-speaking Africans in southern Africa are known to find *Arrow of God* much less interesting, and less relevant, than *Things Fall Apart*. That the novel was too sociologically oriented is proved by the fact the author has found it necessary to cut short or remove some of the traditional stories and songs for the revised edition.

Yet another source of difficulty is the novel's complexity of theme and plot and the large number of characters involved. Achebe tries to contain the whole cultural fabric of Igbo society and the various forces threatening it in one single volume. This necessitates bringing in too many characters to whom the reader must be introduced before he can clearly see who is playing what role in the conflict. Also, many contradictions are involved. From the most general to the most specific we could summarize them as follows:

Culture contact and culture conflict, for example, the colonialists and missionaries versus Umuaro;

Okperi versus Umuaro;

Ezeulu versus his community;

Winterbottom versus his senior officials;

Ezeulu versus Nwaka;

The spiritual side of Ezeulu versus his purely human side (see for instance pp. 191–2).

By the time we come to Chapter Twelve, however, the roles of the main characters are fairly clear; so too is the nature of the main contradictions involved. It is then that Achebe chooses to show us the terrible beauty of Ezeulu's personality; it is then that the author brings in the shock which the people of Umuaro experience, on hearing the white man's messenger violating their canons of linguistic behaviour. The Court messenger arrives soon after Ezeulu and Akuebue have stopped talking about 'weighty things' (p. 135). From now on events gather momentum and plot, language and character interact in making the reader feel the compelling power of the novel.

Arrow of God is not as great a novel as *Things Fall Apart*, but all the same it is a fine achievement. This stems from the appropriateness of the author's choice of language for each of the participants; in the depth of psychological penetration which enables him to create realistic and memorable characters; in the well-constructed plot, and in Achebe's ability to portray culture contact and culture conflict in a powerful, realistic and convincing manner.

Notes

1 See Achebe, *Morning Yet on Creation Day*, p. 55ff.
2 See, for example, B. Lindfors, 'The Palm Oil with which Achebe's Words are Eaten' in *African Literature Today*, No. 1, and Obiechina in his *Culture, Tradition and Society in the West African Novel*.
3 Obiechina, ibid.

6 Ngugi wa Thiong'o — *A Grain of Wheat*

A Grain of Wheat and Earlier Novels

In his earlier novels, *Weep Not, Child* and *The River Between*, Ngugi's style is characterized by simplicity. The simple narrative and descriptive technique of *The River Between* give the book a more or less direct relationship with folk-tales:

> The two ridges lay side by side. One was Kameno, the other was Makuyu. Between them was a valley. It was called the valley of life. Behind Kameno and Makuyu were many more valleys and ridges, lying without any discernible plan. They were like many sleeping lions which never woke. They just slept, the big deep sleep of their creator.   (p. 1)

Such an opening reminds us of the typical story which unfolds gradually in a simple sequence, event following event until we come to the end. The simplicity of narrative is matched by simplicity of texture. In the passage just quoted there is only one complex sentence, and a very short one at that: 'They were like many sleeping lions which never woke.' The second sentence is a compound sentence of the simplest kind. The novel is characterized by the high frequency of short simple sentences, and the texture is so thin that the reader suspects that the simplicity is not wholly a matter of choice — it is a simplicity imposed on the writer by his limitations in vocabulary and syntax. Clarity is a natural consequence of the novel's simplicity of style. There is not much to puzzle the reader as he goes through the book — everything is clearly stated. The same is true of *Weep Not, Child*.

A Grain of Wheat is a far more complex novel, both in style and language. The simple narrative technique has gone; we have moved very far from the structure of traditional stories; and though the texture of the language is in some cases thin, the simplicity of the earlier novels is frequently replaced by a complexity which surpasses what many other writers have written. The first thing that strikes the stylistic critic is a Bible quotation prefixed to the beginning of the first chapter:

> Thou fool, that which thou sowest is not quickened, except it die.
> And that which thou sowest, thou sowest not that body that shall
> be, but bare grain, it may chance of wheat, or of some other
> grain.   I Corinthians 15: 36–7 (p. 1)

References to this and other Bible passages frequently appear in the
novel. If we analyse such references seriously, as we intend to do, we will
realize that the story in *A Grain of Wheat* can be related throughout to
the Bible, so that the total effect of what the novel says is only fully
experienced in relation to the Bible. This is a point we shall come back to.
Meanwhile we shall address ourselves to the first chapter of the book.
These are the opening words:

> Mugo felt nervous. He was lying on his back and looking at the
> roof. Sooty locks hung from the fern and grass thatch and all
> pointed at his heart. A clear drop of water was delicately suspended
> above him. The drop fattened and grew dirtier as it absorbed
> grains of soot. Then it started drawing towards him. He tried to
> shut his eyes. They would not close. He tried to move his head: it
> was firmly chained to the bed-frame. The drop grew larger and
> larger as it drew closer and closer to his eyes. He wanted to cover
> his eyes with his palms; but his hands, his feet, everything refused to
> obey his will. In despair, Mugo gathered himself for a final heave
> and woke up. Now he lay under the blanket and remained
> unsettled fearing, as in the dream, that a drop of cold water would
> suddenly pierce his eyes.   (p. 3)

The technique is significantly different from that of *The River Between*.
Here we are presented with a character who is haunted by a dream in
which a drop of cold water threatens to drop into his eyes, and when we
read the first few sentences we are not very clear about what is
happening. Just as Mugo is initially not aware that he is dreaming, we as
readers are likewise unaware that he is dreaming until we read further.
There are no unusual words and no unusually complicated syntactic
structures here, but the narrative technique can hardly be described as
simple; the reader is required to concentrate a great deal before he can
fully comprehend what is going on.

Tenor of Discourse

As explained in Part 1 a book's tenor of discourse is determined by the
writer's tone of voice and choice of words. In *A Grain of Wheat* the tone is
quite and controlled. Although it is not evident on every single page, the
quiet tone is maintained even where the author describes things that
involve emotions, fear and suffering. There is always the tendency to tone
down the voice, as in the following passage:

One day people in Thabai and Rung'ei woke up to find themselves ringed round with black and white soldiers carrying guns, and tanks last seen on the road during Churchill's war with Hitler. Gunfire smoked in the sky, people held their stomachs. Some men locked themselves in latrines; others hid among the sacks of sugar and beans in the shops. Yet others tried to sneak out of the town towards the forest, only to find that all roads to freedom were blocked. People were being collected into the town-square, the market place, for screening. Gitogo ran to a shop, jumped over the counter, and almost fell onto the shopkeeper whom he found cowering amongst the empty bags. He gesticulated, made puzzled noises, furtively looked and pointed at the soldiers. The shopkeeper in stupid terror stared back blankly at Gitogo. Gitogo suddenly remembered his aged mother sitting alone in the hut. His mind's eye vividly saw scenes of wicked deeds and blood. He rushed out through the back door, and jumped over a fence into the fields, now agitated by the insecurity to which his mother lay exposed. Urgency, home, mother: the images flashed through his mind. His muscles alone would protect her. He did not see that a whiteman, in a bush jacket, lay camouflaged, in a small wood. 'Halt!' the whiteman shouted. Gitogo continued running. Something hit him at the back. He raised his arms in the air. He fell on his stomach. Apparently the bullet had touched his heart. The soldier left his place. Another Mau Mau terrorist had been shot dead.   (p. 6)

The passage deals with violence, horror and intense suffering, but the tone is matter of fact and quiet. Here people are forced to suppress their feelings. The old woman does not go shouting about the death of her beloved son who has been shot: her son, the deaf and dumb one who could hardly pose any threat to the white man. Her control of her feelings is reflected in the language itself. There is so much suffering, so much pain, that reticence and not shouting is the only way to express what one feels deep down: 'When the old woman heard the news she merely said: My God. Those who were present said that she did not weep. Or even ask how her son had met his death' (p. 6).

The understatement and quietness of the tone come out in the use of such expressions as 'something hit him at the back', 'the bullet had touched his heart'. To the victims of this violence, the experience is terrible, but to the white man who does the shooting the death and pain of 'the African rebel' is an achievement; so he has no feelings, killing a 'terrorist' evokes no emotions in him. This coldness and lack of feeling for the victim of the gun is expressed in the tone of the language: 'Another Mau Mau terrorist had been shot dead'. The point of view expressed here is that of a Government official, which the reader cannot be in sympathy with; for he is aware that Gitogo is not a terrorist but a poor son compelled by filial love to go and protect his aged mother from the terror of the white man's soldiers.

Another good example of Ngugi's control of tone is the passage which depicts Gikonyo's disappointment with Mumbi on his return from detention. He has betrayed the people's cause by confessing the oath — he has done this because he thought that he could sacrifice anything in order to live with his family, with Mumbi; that paragon of purity and incorruptibility he so clearly visualized in his mind when he was in detention, only to find on his arrival home that Mumbi has born a child to his rival and enemy, Karanja, the white man's lackey. The painful self-control, the resigned manner in which Gikonyo receives the news is expressed in the language:

> 'I'm tired, mother. I have come a long way and I want to sleep,' he said. Wangari did not understand. And now Mumbi wept.
>
> He failed to sleep. Gikonyo lay on his back and stared into the darkness, every minute conscious of the heavy breathing from the two women. Six years he had waited for this day; six years through seven detention camps had he longed for it, feeling, all the time, that life's meaning was contained in his final return to Mumbi. Nothing else had mattered: the camps, mountains, valleys, everything could have been wiped from the face of the earth and Gikonyo would have watched this, without flinching, if he had known that he would, in the end, go back to the woman he had left behind. Little did he then think, never thought it could ever be a return to silence. Could the valley of silence between him and the woman be now crossed? To what end the crossing since he would reach the other side to find a woman who had hardly waited for him to disappear round the corner, before she rushed back to bed with another man? No, this silence was eternal.   (pp. 100–1)

There is no doubt here that the man is hurt, disappointed, and bitter; but the hurt, the disappointment and the bitterness are so intensely felt that the expression of them is painfully controlled. The quietness and gentleness of the language moves the reader and makes this a very touching passage indeed.

The control of language and tone extends to the writer's treatment of sex and to physical appetites and taboos generally. In the dialogue, there is less control, as is appropriate to the character speaking. For example, Githua, that hilarious cripple, has the guts to say: 'I was not always like that. I swear by my mother's aged cunt, or that of the old woman' (p. 109). And Koinandu talking of a white woman, Dr Lynd, says to his fellows: 'Man I'll break her in. I'll swim in that hole' (p. 185). This is bawdy, but the author is merely recording realistically what a man of Githua's or Koinandu's turn of mind would have said in the circumstances, and so we cannot charge Ngugi with indecency. His reticence in sexual matters is exemplified by the following passage where he describes how two women found Mugo passing water:

> He dug a little, and feeling the desire to pass water, walked to a
> hedge near the path ... He found his bladder had pressed him into
> false urgency. A few drops trickled down and he watched them as if
> each drop fascinated him. Two young women dressed for church,
> passed near, saw a big man playing with his thing and giggled.
> Mugo felt foolish and dragged himself back to his work.   (p. 7)

The expression 'feeling the desire to pass water' is typically polite and
free from heavy connotations. We notice the avoidance of even a
common word like 'urine' in the passage. There is instead a reference to 'a
few drops'. In the same way, Mugo's organ is referred to as 'his thing'
according to the canons of linguistic behaviour in the two women's
society.

Ngugi does not refrain from describing in realistic language the
grosser aspects of human life and human behaviour. Just as he is capable
of describing the various aspects of the sex act, he does not hide the fact
that man removes waste matter from his body by passing stools, as the
following passage shows:

> He excused himself and went towards the latrine. Run away from
> all these men ... He entered the pit lavatory and lowered his
> trousers to his knees: his thoughts buzzed around flashing images
> of his visitors seated in the hut. Several times he tried to force
> something out into the smelling pit. Failing, he pulled up his
> trousers, but still he felt better for the effort. He went back to the
> visitors and only now remembered that he had not greeted
> them.   (pp. 9–10)

There is a balance here between realism and modesty.

In describing the sex act, Ngugi uses language that makes the reader
see beauty and grace in it, as opposed to the shock or even disgust that a
reader may feel when reading other writers. This is exemplified in the
following passage:

> 'Mumbi, —' he tried to say something as he held her to himself. She
> lay against his breast, their heart-beat each to each. It was all quiet.
> Mumbi was trembling, and this sent a quiver of fear and joy trilling
> in his blood. Gradually, he pulled her to the ground, the long grass
> covered them. Mumbi breathed hard, but could not, dare not,
> speak. One by one, Gikonyo removed her clothes as if performing a
> dark ritual in the wood. Now her body gleamed in the sun. Her
> eyes were soft and wild and submissive and defiant. Gikonyo
> passed his hands through her hair and over her breasts, slowly
> coaxing and smoothing stiffness from her body, until she lay limp
> in his hands. Suddenly, Gikonyo found himself suspended in a
> void, he was near breaking point and as he swooned into the dark
> depth he heard a moan escape Mumbi's parted lips. She held him
> tight to herself. Their breath was now one. The earth moved
> beneath their one body into a stillness.   (p. 80)

The tenderness and overpowering emotional excitement which lovers feel at their first encounter, and the transcendental pleasure of a couple united physically and totally, their souls fused in the sweetness of their trance; this is all reflected with grace and dignity. The tenderness of love and irresistible power of desire are reflected in that one word, 'Mumbi'. The silence that is imposed on the couple by the language of their emotions comes out in these sentences: 'Mumbi breathed hard, but could not, dare not, speak. One by one ... Gikonyo passed his hands through her hair and over her breasts, slowly coaxing and smoothing stiffness from her body, until she lay limp in his hands.' The author's reticence is demonstrated by his avoidance of loaded words. We know of course that Gikonyo's exploring hand would not have stopped at Mumbi's hair and breasts, but Ngugi withholds the rest of the information and spares us from the shock of the mentioning of the unmentionable. Unlike Armah, he does not delight in recreating the rhythms of sex; he is content with describing in abstract terms the transformation of the lovers into a physical union of joy, forgetful of themselves and this world. Instead of being told directly about Gikonyo experiencing an orgasm, we are told that he was 'near breaking point' and 'swooned into the dark depth'.

Ngugi the Psychologist

A Grain of Wheat is above all a book which deals with the effects of great events of the external world on individual people. The events portrayed take place in the context of the Mau Mau war and the coming of Uhuru, but the writer focuses our attention not on the events as abstractions, but on their effects on the individual soul and the individual mind, and on person-to-person relationships. There is, for instance, Thompson, the colonial administrator; there is Karanja, to all intents and purposes a slave of the white man, believing that the white man is all-powerful and cannot loosen his hold on the reins of power in Kenya; and there is Mugo who has betrayed the leader of the freedom fighters, Kihika. To all these people the coming of Uhuru has diverse and complex effects.

Thompson had once believed so much in the greatness and worth of British imperialism that he declared: 'In a flash I was convinced that the growth of the British Empire was the development of a great moral idea: it means, it must surely lead to the creation of one British nation, embracing people of all colours and creeds, based on the just proposition that all men were created equal' (p. 48). But Thompson is destined to see the end of British rule in Kenya, and when preparations for Uhuru are under way, he reflects on what he has believed in and what is to come:

> No matter how he looked at it, Thompson was pinched by sadness at the knowledge that the Duke would sit to see the flag lowered, never to rise again on this side of Albion's shore. This sadness was accentuated by his mind racing back to 1952 when the Queen, then a princess, visited Kenya. For a minute, Thompson forgot the

newspaper and relived that moment when the young woman shook hands with him. He was then District Officer. He felt a thrill: his heart-beat had quickened almost as if a covenant had been made between him and her. Then, there, he would have done anything for her, would have stabbed himself to prove his readiness to carry out that mission which though unspoken seemed embodied in her person and smile. Recalling that rapture, Thompson involuntarily pushed away the paper and rose to his feet. There was a flicker in his eyes, a watery glint. He walked towards the window muttering under his breath:

'What the hell was it all about!'   (pp. 37–8)

By using the omniscient narrator technique, Ngugi gives himself the power to enter the minds of his characters and probe their deepest thoughts. In the passage just quoted, he penetrates into the mind of a disappointed colonial officer. Elsewhere he penetrates into the minds of the suffering, the mentally tortured and those on the verge of mental derangement. A good example of the last mentioned is the passage which describes Mugo's behaviour to Mumbi when she is sent to persuade him to speak on Uhuru day:

> She tried to cry out for help, but no voice would leave her throat. He came towards her, emitting demented noises and laughter. She bounded to the door; but he was there before her.
>
> 'You cannot — run away. Sit down — Ha! I will do it to you —'
> He was shaking and his words came out in violent jerks.
>
> 'Imagine all your life cannot sleep — so many fingers touching your flesh — eyes watching you — in dark places — in corners — in the streets — in the fields — sleeping, waking, no rest — ah! Those eyes — cannot you for a minute, one minute, leave a man alone — I mean — let a man eat, drink, work — all of you — Kihika — Gikonyo — the old woman — that general — who sent you here tonight? Who? Aah! Those eyes again — we shall see who is stronger — now —'
>
> She tried to scream, again no voice would come out. He closed in on her, one hand on her mouth, the other searching her throat. She panted and whimpered horribly. She looked into his eyes. Even later she could not explain the terror she saw in them. And all of a sudden she ceased struggling and submitted herself to him.
>
> 'What is it, Mugo? What is wrong?' she sobbed.   (pp. 161–2)

The writer attempts here to capture, through linguistic technique, the mind of a man haunted by guilt. The language in its jerks and broken rhythms, reflects not only the way Mugo thought and spoke on this occasion, but also the crushing guilt that had dogged him since the betrayal of Kihika. The hallucinations of his tortured mind are vividly portrayed. Mugo is here like Macbeth who is constantly haunted by the

ghost of Banquo whom he has murdered. He feels watched by everybody
—by the dead and by the living, by Kihika, Gikonyo, the old woman, the
general. The horror that he experiences is passed on to Mumbi who is
completely overtaken by terror; she too is transported into an unknown
world and cannot understand what is going on. Through his use of
language Ngugi wants us too to experience something of what Mugo
and Mumbi have experienced, and when the rapture is over we are
brought back to reality, to the present, by Mumbi's question: '"What is
it, Mugo? What is wrong?" she sobbed.'

Ngugi's psychological penetration is part and parcel of his tendency to
abstract. With Achebe we hardly think in terms of abstract things. His
style is concrete, his characters are developed through a process of
conversation, acting, and thinking about concrete things. Not so Ngugi's
characters: they are capable of riding on the waves of abstract thinking
and the author has the ability to recreate such abstract thinking in fit
words. Take this passage for example:

> Mugo stared at a pole opposite; he tried to grasp the sense of what
> Gikonyo had said. He had always found it difficult to make
> decisions. Recoiling as if by instinct from setting in motion a course
> of action whose consequences he could not determine before the
> start, he allowed himself to drift into things or be pushed into them
> by an uncanny demon; he rode on the wave of circumstance and
> lay against the crest, fearing but fascinated by fate. Something of
> that devilish fascination now seemed to light his eyes. His body was
> deathly still.   (p. 23)

The passage opens with the contemplation of a concrete thing, a pole,
and then we gradually move into the abstract in short sentences where
such words as 'grasp the sense of' and 'to make decisions' refer to mental
processes and immaterial things, before we plunge into the depth of
abstractness in the third sentence which depends for its effect on length,
on the undulating rhythm and on the choice of word and phrase. The
beauty of the sentence is partly the result of the writer's use of words
which refer to motion: 'setting in motion', 'drift into things', 'rode on the
wave of circumstance', 'lay against the crest'. As usual, we are brought
back to the present by a question: ' "What do you say?" Wambui asked,
slightly impatient with Mugo's intense look ...' The effect of this shift is
to create a sharp contrast between the abstract and the concrete,
between the abstractions of the mind and the actualities of the present.
Mugo's reflection takes us far away into the dark regions of his mind;
Wambui's question and explanation brings us back to the events of the
day.

Biblical References

The quotations from and references to the Bible function on two levels.
At one level we are led to think mainly of the symbolic significance of

Ngugi's use of the Bible; at another level the language of the Bible and of religion in general becomes an object of analysis in its own right; it becomes a variety of language which contributes to the internal stylistic features of the novel. Where extracts from the Bible function at the level of para-linguistic affective devices, our main focus is not on the analysis of the minute linguistic features of each extract, but on the total effect which the extract has on the novel, on its affectiveness and semantic significance; for by relating some of the key extracts to the events in the novel we get a deeper insight into the novel than we would otherwise. Take, for instance the first quotation from I Corinthians 15: 36–7:

> Thou fool, that which thou sowest is not quickened, except it die. And that which thou sowest, thou sowest not that body that shall be, but bare grain, it may chance of wheat, or of some other grain.   (p. 1)

The general significance of this quotation should be seen in terms of the story of *A Grain of Wheat*. This includes incidents relating to the days of the struggle for national liberation, when the sons and daughter of Kenya suffered and even died for freedom's sake. The quotation can therefore be taken to stand for the idea that if Kenyans were to achieve their independence, they had to sow seeds which would die in order to bear grain. In other words, Kenya had to bring forth heroes who were prepared to die so that the rest of the nation would find life. This is the meaning of the quotation on a general level.

But it also has a particular significance. The quotation from Corinthians should be read in the context of what happens in the first two chapters of the book, where we learn about Kihika who dies during the struggle for liberation. This interpretation is borne out by the last two paragraphs of the second chapter:

> Kihika was hanged in public, one Sunday, at Rung'ei Market, not far from where he had once stood calling for blood to rain on and water the tree of freedom. A combined force of Homeguards and Police whipped and drove people from Thabai and other ridges to see the body of the rebel dangling on the tree, and learn.
>
> The Party, however, remained alive and grew, as people put it, on the wounds of those Kihika left behind.   (p. 17)

Kihika here becomes a suffering saviour. He is hanged in public like Christ and sheds his blood that all may be free. He becomes the seed that is sown and dies. The grain that comes out is seen in the growth of the Party which continues to flourish after Kihika's death. Read in the light of the Bible quotation, therefore, the last two paragraphs of the second chapter assume a far greater significance than at first meets the eye.

The Corinthians quotation is the first of what I call external references to the Bible, those which are not part of the text but are affixed to the beginning of chapters. The chapters in question are Chapter One,

Chapter Four, Chapter Nine and Chapter Fourteen. The second
quotation is the second of the verses underlined in Kihika's little Bible:

> And the Lord spoke unto Moses,
> Go unto Pharaoh, and say unto him,
> Thus saith the Lord,
> Let my people go.   Exodus 8: 1 (p. 29)

The quotation refers to the liberation of the people of Kenya. The
theme of the deliverance of the children of Israel is transferred from its
Bible context to the Kenyan situation, where there is a struggle for the
liberation of the people of Kenya from British imperialism. Kihika has
the duty to go to the colonialists and declare: 'Let my people go'. This is
the way Ngugi uses the Bible in the novel. The Bible myth which is well
known to Ngugi's readers, is adapted and given a political significance.
But more about this later; for the time being we might note that while the
relationship between the Exodus passage first quoted and the text may
seem too indirect, we do have a clear reference to Moses in Chapter Eight
where, thinking about the visit of Gikonyo and General K to him the
previous night, Mugo begins to entertain the idea that he might be a
Moses sent to save the people of his land:

> For he walked on the edge of a revelation: Gikonyo and Githua
> had brought him there. He remembered the words: he shall save
> the children of the needy. It must be him. It was he, Mugo, spared
> to save people like Githua, the old woman, and any who had
> suffered. Why not take the task? Yes. He would speak at the Uhuru
> celebrations ... It was so in the time of Jacob and Esau; it was so in
> the time of Moses.   (p. 110)

The interesting thing is that a reader who is going through the novel
for the first time may take Mugo's revelations seriously and think that
Mugo has a special mission to fulfil in his society. The reader shares
Mugo's illusion until, later in the book, it becomes very clear that Mugo
betrayed the real Moses, Kihika. Thus taken in relation to the specific
context of Chapter Eight, the verse from Exodus is ironical. Mugo is not
a saviour but a Judas, the betrayer of Kihika the true saviour.

The third external reference to the Bible is, like the second, also from
Exodus, and is also one of the verses underlined in Kihika's Bible:

> And the Lord said, I have surely seen the affliction of my people
> which are in Egypt, and have heard their cry by reason of their task
> masters; for I know their sorrows.   Exodus 3: 7 (p. 113)

This is a passage about a suffering people and here Egypt becomes, in the
context of Kenya, the colonial situation, while the affliction of the Lord's
people can be seen to relate to the suffering of the people during the
Emergency. It is this suffering which Mumbi describes to Mugo in
Chapter Nine where she tells him about the whipping and torture which

led to the singing of sorrowful songs such as the following:

> When I remember Wambuku
> A woman who was beautiful so
> How she raised her eyes to heaven
> Tears from the heart freely flow.
> Pray true
> Praise Him true
> For He is ever the same God.
> Who will forget the sun and the dust today
> And the trench I dug with blood!
> When they pushed me into the trench,
> Tears from my heart freely flowed.   (p. 126)

It is a moving song sung by a suffering people, and the narrative comment on the song uses words of compassion and beauty:

> Mumbi had stopped her narrative to hum the tunes for Mugo, trying to fit in two words she had forgotten. The tunes were slow, defiant, yet mournful, and tears clearly stood at the edges of her eyes. Her breasts rose and fell with the songs, and Mugo was rooted to his seat, painfully reliving a scene he never saw, for by that time he had been detained.   (pp. 126–7)

The fourth and fifth extracts are on p. 175. The first seems to be a fulfillment of the Corinthians verse at the beginning of the book; for while the Corinthians extract points to the need for some people to die in order that salvation may come to the rest, this passage goes beyond the need for sacrifice and points positively to the fruit that results from the sacrifice:

> Verily, verily I say unto you, Except a corn of wheat fall into the ground and die, it abideth alone: but if it die, it bringeth forth much fruit.   St John 12: 24

This is complemented by the Revelation passage:

> And I saw a new heaven and a new earth: for the first heaven and the first earth were passed away.   Revelation 21: 1

These two verses look forward to the birth of a new nation, to the coming of Uhuru. While the first promises 'much fruit' emanating from the sufferings of a people who have fought for their freedom, the second looks forward to the coming of 'a new heaven and a new earth' and to the passing away of the old. When we open the next page to read the first words of Chapter Fourteen we come face to face with the new heaven, the new earth, for here independent Kenya is coming into being while British rule is coming to an end:

> Kenya regained her Uhuru from the British on 12 December 1963.
> A minute before midnight, lights were put out at the Nairobi

stadium so that people from all over the country and the world who had gathered there for the midnight ceremony were swallowed by the darkness. In the dark, the Union Jack was quickly lowered. When next the lights came on the new Kenya flag was flying and fluttering, and waving, in the air.   (p. 177)

The use of the language of the Bible to express a political theme is clearly demonstrated in some of the references in the actual text. The first example we shall cite is a passage extracted from one of Kihika's political speeches. Karanja has just accused him of inconsistency: 'This morning you said Jesus had failed', says Karanja in a contemptuous tone, 'And now you say we need Christ ...' To this Kihika replies:

'Yes — I said he had failed because his death did not change anything, it did not make his people find a centre in the cross. All oppressed people have a cross to bear. The Jews refused to carry it and were scattered like dust all over the earth. Had Christ's death a meaning for the children of Israel? In Kenya we want a death which will change things, that is to say, we want a true sacrifice. But first we have to be ready to carry the cross. I die for you, you die for me, we become a sacrifice for one another. So I can say that you, Karanja, are Christ. I am Christ. Everybody who takes the Oath of Unity to change things in Kenya is a Christ.'   (p. 83)

The shift from the Bible to the struggle, from religion to politics, is quite clear. The cross is now a political cross, a Christ is he who fights for the freedom of the people. The Christian message is transformed into a mwssage for political liberation. This passage is in fact a key to Ngugi's attitude to the situation in Kenya. Moreover, it provides us with an instance of his use of irony in the novel. 'In Kenya we want a death which will change things', says Kihika. The question to ask is: what change is there in Kenya when Uhuru comes? Does Kihika's own death change things in Kenya, and does the coming of Uhuru? In the last chapter of the book the writer tells us that Kenya regained her Uhuru on 12 December 1963, but the impression the reader gets is that, despite the celebration, there is nevertheless no sense of victory, no satisfaction that things have changed for the better. The one positive result that has been achieved is the reconciliation of Gikonyo and Mumbi — symbolic perhaps that the gods torn apart by the struggle are now united.[1] As regards the lot of the peasants who suffered for Uhuru, the reader is reminded of the note at the beginning of the book: 'But the situation and the problems are real — sometimes too painfully real for the peasants who fought the British yet who now see all they fought for being put on one side' (p. vi). The peasants therefore met disappointment rather than adequate recompense for the sacrifices they made. There are examples of this in the book. When Gikonyo goes to see the MP for Thabai about a loan, he is ignored; and the honourable Member does not so much as turn up for the village celebrations: he neglects the people who have voted for him.

Not only that, he deprives Gikonyo and his group of the farm they wanted to buy. The only way the poor can express their disappointment with such ministers is in Warui's words: 'They'll only raise wrath against the hearts of their worshippers' (p. 149).

Read in this light, the Bible quotations attached to the last chapter of the book are nothing but ironical. The quotation from St John talks about 'a corn of wheat' dying and bringing forth much fruit. If the corn referred to is Kihika and all those heroes who died for Kenyan independence, then there is not much fruit that came up as a result. The second quotation is about 'a new heaven and a new earth'. A Kenyan peasant who is disappointed with the type of Uhuru that has been achieved may well ask: 'What new heaven and new earth is there? Is this the heaven and earth we suffered for?' Gikonyo had dreamt of a land of glory and plenty. When soldiers came to take him to detention he had accepted his fate happily for he thought that 'the day would come, indeed was near at hand when he would rejoin Thabai and, together with those who had taken to the forest, would rock the earth with a new song at the birth of freedom' (pp. 90–91).

The very title of the book, *A Grain of Wheat*, should be read in the light of what we have discussed. It is an ironic reference to the political situation in Kenya. Many grains of wheat fell into the ground and died, but did they sprout? And did they bring forth much fruit?

The use of Biblical references and the language of the Bible has a special significance for the character Mugo. Mugo sees himself as a Moses sent to redeem the sons of Israel. He has a vision which the reader is tempted to share, until it becomes clear that Mugo is the one who betrayed Kihika. Ngugi represents Mugo's vision with skill and power, turning the mind of the reader from the Bible to the novel, from Moses to Mugo, from the children of Israel to the people of Kenya. Here is one good example:

> Mugo lay on his back under the shade of a Mwariki and experienced that excessive contentment which one feels during a noon rest from toil. A voice, then he always heard voices whenever he lay on his back at rest, told him: something is going to happen to you. Closing his eyes, he could feel, almost touched the thing, whose form was vague but, oh, so beautiful. He let the gentle voice lure him to distant lands in the past. Moses too was alone keeping the flock of Jethro his father-in-law. And he led the flock to the far side of the desert, and came to the mountain of God, even to Horeb. And the angel of the Lord appeared unto him in a flame of fire out of the midst of a bush. And God called out to him in a thin voice, Moses, Moses: And Mugo cried out, Here am I, Lord.   (p. 108)

The sudden shift from Moses to Mugo in those last two sentences is specially effective.

Ngugi can also parody the language of the Bible and the language of religious fanatics in an amusing way. A good example of this is the passage describing Jackson's conversion and his manner of preaching. Here Ngugi catches the tone of the Preacher in the Bible, and imitates at the same time Ecclesiastes and the rhetoric of modern religious fanatics with amazing accuracy:

> A few months after the State of Emergency was declared, Jackson suddenly became converted to this movement. He stood in front of the congregation at Mahiga and like a man possessed, trembled and beat his breast, saying: 'I had called myself a Christian. I had put a white collar around my neck and thought this would save me from the fire to come. Vanity of vanities, saith the preacher, vanity of vanities. All was vanity. For my heart harboured anger, pride, jealousy, theft and adulterous thoughts. My company was with drunkards and adulterers. I walked in the darkness and waded through the mud of sins. I had not seen Jesus. I had not found the light. Then, on the night of 12 January 1953, I was suddenly struck by the thunderbolt of the Lord, and I cried: Lord, what shall I do to be saved? And he took my hands and thrust them into his side and I saw the print of the nails in his hands. And I cried again: Lord, wash me in thy blood. And he said: Jackson, follow me.' Then he confessed how he used to minister unto the devil: by eating, drinking and laughing with sinners; by being too soft with the village elders and those who had rejected Christ; by not letting Christ's blood water the seed so that it could take root. He was now a Christian soldier, marching as to war; politics was dirty, worldly wealth a sin.   (p. 74)

The self-righteousness of Jackson and the likes of him comes out very clearly. The tenor of discourse shows that Ngugi is poking fun at the fanaticism of Jackson and his followers. We as readers are neither convinced nor impressed by Jackson's argument and enthusiasm, and we are not convinced that he is now a true Christian soldier 'marching as to war', and that what he condemns as dirty and sinful (politics and wealth) are really dirty and sinful things. The exaggerated enthusiasm for religion and the fanatical nature of the confession are portrayed by the very rhythm and movement of the language: 'I had called myself a Christian. I had put a white collar around my neck ...' Note the repetition of 'I had' and the enthusiasm reflected in the reiteration of the word 'vanity'. The exaggerated enthusiasm is paralleled by the hyperbolical language. Strong and extravagant metaphors are used. His heart 'harboured anger, pride, jealousy, theft and adulterous thoughts'. His company was with 'drunkards and adulterers'; he walked in the darkness and 'waded through the mud of sin'; he was 'suddenly struck by the thunderbolt of the Lord'. These extravagant metaphors show a lack of genuine conviction and a puerile mind.

Historical Narrative

One interesting feature of Ngugi's narrative technique is that now and again he shifts from the conventional style of the writer of fiction to that of a historian or biographer. He opens a paragraph or a chapter with a comment about an actual event in the struggle for Uhuru. Sometimes he speaks as if he is addressing a group of people around him, in a tone showing familiarity with his audience. This is how Chapter Nine opens:

> Learned men will, no doubt, dig into the troubled times which we in Kenya underwent, and maybe sum up the lesson of history in a phrase. Why, let us ask them, did the incident in Rira Camp capture the imagination of the world? For there were other camps, bigger, scattered all over Kenya, from the Manda Islands in the Indian Ocean to the Magata Islands in Lake Victoria.   (p. 115)

In this passage the reader is temporarily transported from the world of fiction to the world of historical fact. A non-historian who is not familiar with the details of detention camps during the Emergency in Kenya may well ask: Is Ngugi describing a simple fact or is Rira Camp a fictitious camp invented by Ngugi so that he may appear to be narrating actual historial events? Is the reference to 'the imagination of the world' a fact or is it simply Ngugi's method of simulating reality?

Chapter Thirteen is another example. This is how it opens:

> Most of us from Thabai first saw him at the New Rung'ei Market the day the heavy rain fell. You remember the Wednesday, just before Independence? Wind blew and the rain hit the ground at an angle. Women abandoned their wares in the open and scampered to the shops for shelter ...   (p. 155)

Ngugi achieves this sense of closeness to his audience by identifying himself as one of 'us from Thabai', and by addressing the reader as 'you'. To make his narrative more like a recording of actual historical events, the author–narrator goes on to refer to the return of Kenyatta home from England, and to the Kenyan leader's return to Gatundu from Maralal. The reference to Kenyatta ties up with the first sentence: 'Most of us from Thabai saw him'. There is sufficient ambiguity on this page to confuse the reader as to whether the hero referred to is Kenyatta or Mugo. That 'the man walk(ing) in the rain' is intended to be Mugo can be inferred from the fact that Mugo has a guilty conscience. Walking and drenching himself in the rain is a way of expiating the guilt of having betrayed the saviour of the people. Hence one of the bystanders remarks: 'Or maybe he has something heavy in his heart' (p. 155). The association of Mugo with Kenyatta here has the effect of building up Mugo into a towering giant:

> We saw the man walk in the rain. An old dirty basket filled with vegetables and potatoes was slung on his back. He was tall, with

broad shoulders, and he walked with a slight stoop that created an impression of power. The fact that he was the only man in the rain soon attracted the attention of people along the pavements and shop verandahs. Some even forced their way to the front to see him.   (p. 155)

This technique of bringing together fact and fiction comes out very clearly in the last chapter where actual historical facts surrounding the coming of Uhuru are fused with the fiction of the events which took place in Thabai (see p. 177 ff). The opening sentences could be from any authentic historical account of the coming of independence in Kenya. The date is given, including the day, the month, the year. The details of the lowering of the Union Jack and the raising of the new flag are given. And when we are introduced to the village celebrations in the next paragraph, the description of what happened sounds real and immediate.

Ngugi and his Characters — the Flashback

All the aspects of Ngugi's style discussed here should be seen in relation to the writer's technique of the flashback.[2] Events are not told chronologically in the novel. There is a constant shift from the present to the past, from the present to the future. Information about characters and events is given and withheld so that it is not easy to make a final judgement about a character until the very end. The reader is indeed tempted to pass judgement on characters all along, but judgement is likely to be wrong if not deferred until the end. Githua, that hilarious character, convinces Mugo and the reader that he lost his leg in the struggle for independence, until more information is given about him later in the book (see pp. 132–3). As for Mugo, the reader finds him mysterious and may at times be convinced that he is a saviour, a Moses sent to lead the people of Thabai to freedom. The terrible information about his betrayal of Kihika comes after he has been built up as a hero.

Exploiting the technique of the flashback, Ngugi writes a moving story, full of sympathy for the characters. All the characters in the novel are riddled with faults. Mugo, the great hero in the eyes of the people of Thabai, turns out to be a traitor. Gikonyo confesses the oath. Mumbi, the epitome of beauty and feminine love, is given a child by her husband's arch-enemy, Karanja. For his part, Karanja takes upon himself the role of a traitor to his people, the white man's lackey and willing instrument in the oppression of the African.

And yet each of these characters is presented with such compassion that the reader does not condemn their weaknesses, but accepts them as the shortcomings of real people. The only exception to this sympathetic presentation are the white officials of the colonial administration, particularly Thompson. Thompson stands for outlandish colonial ideals and is on the side of those who have oppressed and tortured the people and freedom-fighters. Little sympathy is shown for him.

Aesthetic Qualities

In *A Grain of Wheat*, Ngugi uses Standard English and uses it well. There is no attempt to Africanize the language, as we find in Okara and Achebe — though a few Swahili words like *Uhuru* and *harambee* are used. There is no linguistic virtuosity, the reader is not held back by unusual words, and Ngugi has a feel of word and phrase which is entirely satisfactory. Words are not wasted, the language is compact.

In terms of varieties of language, the novel is limited. In choosing Standard English, Ngugi has deliberately shunned the linguistic experiments of Achebe and Okara, who both try to reflect African modes of thinking. In consequence, linguistic differentiation as a method of depicting characters is minimal in *A Grain of Wheat*. There is no noticeable difference between the language of Gikonyo and that of Mugo, Mumbi or even Karanja. The question of their educational or social background is irrelevant. Whether educated or uneducated Ngugi's characters speak meticulous English, the language of the author. Whether the writer is translating or quoting his speakers verbatim are not questions that cross our minds as we read through the book. There are, however two exceptions. The language of Thompson is clearly marked off from the language of other characters because Thompson is not a very likeable character and his whole philosophy and attitude to the politics of Kenya is unacceptable. He is the prototype of an English colonial. It is therefore his ideas and attitude, as well as his tone of voice, which set Thompson apart from the rest of the characters in the novel. He is Ngugi's version of Captain Winterbottom, yet the quality of his English is not significantly different from that of uneducated characters like Mumbi. The other exception is Githua. He is so funny and bawdy that he is linguistically differentiated from the others.

If any African novel has a claim to complexity, it is *A Grain of Wheat*. Of the books treated in this volume, only *Two Thousand Seasons* can by virtue of its ambitious theme, claim a higher degree of complexity. Though the language itself is not laboured and complicated, Ngugi's narrative technique is sufficiently complex to make the book one of the most sophisticated in the African literature so far published. If the narrative structure is complex, the response it calls forth in the reader is equally complex. The reader's attitude to characters and his impressions about the thread of events keep on shifting as the narrative shifts from one person to another, from one event to another, from one focus to another. He may dislike a character in one part of the novel, but in the next he may like him better, or at least learn to understand or accept the character's faults. The characters themselves get a better understanding of themselves and others, of their own motives and other people's motives, as the story progresses to its end. Thus our feelings towards Mumbi change as we get a better understanding of the circumstances which led to her having a child with Karanja, and Gikonyo himself acquires a better understanding of Mumbi in the end; he finally learns to accept a new relationship between himself and his wife, who is now a new person to him.

To sum up, *A Grain of Wheat* is a fine achievement: the compactness and clarity of language, the writer's ability to reflect what goes on in the human mind, the superb use of flashbacks, the controlled narrative, the sophisticated use of Biblical references, the compassion with which human faults are depicted — all these combine to make an excellent book, linguistically and structurally, and one whose depth of human concern is at once realistic and moving.

Notes

1 See Dathorne, *African Literature in the Twentieth Century*, p. 129.
2 Ngugi's use of the flashback is discussed in detail in Palmer's *An Introduction to the African Novel.*

7 Wole Soyinka — *Season of Anomy*

▼▼▼▼▼▼▼▼▼▼▼▼▼▼▼▼▼▼▼▼▼▼▼▼▼▼▼▼▼▼▼▼

Theme and Symbolism

Season of Anomy is Soyinka's second novel. It was published in 1973, eight years after its predecessor, *The Interpreters*. Critics have claimed Soyinka's non-alignment to any specific ideology, but in *Season of Anomy* Soyinka comes very close to a commitment to socialist ideals.[1] The author may not consider himself committed to socialism, but his work can certainly be given a socialist interpretation. Ernst Fischer has said: 'Socialist art and literature as a whole imply the artist's or writer's fundamental agreement with the aims of the working class and the emerging socialist world.'[2] In *Season of Anomy* there is a definite antithesis between monopoly capitalism and repression on the one hand and progressive communalism on the other. Monopoly capitalism is represented by the Cartel Corporation and the Mining Trust, and as monopoly capitalism must protect itself against the wrath of the exploited masses, we see an unholy alliance coming into existence, an alliance between 'the purse and the gun'. The regime running the affairs of the country (which could be Nigeria or any other African state) is a military regime. The Cartel itself is propped up by four distinguished personages: Chief Batoki, Chief Biga, Zaki Amuri and the Commandant-in-Chief who declares that the hope for 'national stability' is in 'the alliance of the purse and the gun' (p. 138). The forces of progress are represented at the most elementary level by the communalist ideals of Aiyéró (p. 2 ff) and on a higher level by Ofeyi's idea of a community of workers breaking down the artificial frontiers of tribe and region and undermining the exploitative activities of the Cartel. The idea is summarized in the following sentence: 'The goals were clear enough, the dream a new concept of labouring hands across artificial frontiers, the concrete, affective presence of Aiyéró throughout the land, undermining the Cartel's superstructure of robbery, indignities and murder, ending the new phase of slavery' (p. 27). Ofeyi would like to work with the men of Aiyéró because 'they live by an idea' (p. 27). Ofeyi's idea eventually merges with that of Demakin, the Dentist, who believes in the systematic elimination of the chief members of the group of exploiters.

The confrontation between the two forces described above can be more fully understood by studying Soyinka's use of a sophisticated form of para-linguistic affective device — the use of subtitles with an implied but hidden meaning. The book is divided into five parts, entitled: 'Seminal', 'Buds', 'Tentacles', 'Harvest', and 'Spores'. An examination of these titles in sequence, relating each to the content of the chapters included under it, will reveal something of the dialectical relationship between the two contradictory forces.

We are first introduced to Aiyéró's communalism, and then Ofeyi comes in and gets inspired by the idea. By the time we come to the end of 'Seminal II' we are left in no doubt that Ofeyi has the progressive idea already referred to. He has also come round to the view that violence may be necessary in a revolution: 'Just the same, the sowing of any idea these days can no longer take place without accepting the need to protect the young seedling, even by violent means' (p. 23). We therefore see the genesis of a strategy whose ultimate aim is to destroy exploitation, and this is what is symbolized by the title 'Seminal'. At the same time, the Cartel is beginning to awaken to the need to suppress any form of opposition to the system it represents. Ofeyi, for instance, has already been sent on a study tour in the hope that by being exposed to the capitalist world — America, Japan, Germany — he might yet be won over to toe the Cartel line (pp. 20–1).

In 'Buds' Ofeyi begins to be much more than a thorn in the flesh of the Cartel. His activities cause both the Corporation and the Government 'very great concern' (p. 53). Among other things he writes satirical songs to be sung by Zaccheus' band, and satirizes the four bigmen of the Corporation in the pandora's box display. The Corporation's Trouble-shooter who is called upon to deal with him indirectly accuses him of being an agitator, a communist, a Marxist and a socialist (p. 55). The Trouble-shooter is a representative of the Commandant who is the local Government Official. Like the Chairman of the Corporation (and no doubt like his Government bosses) he is opposed to socialism or anything to do with Moscow (p. 55). During the interrogation, Ofeyi openly champions the cause of the workers who are apparently being killed for demanding justice: 'What we don't know is where the workers disappear to, the so-called agitators' (p. 54). As he escapes from the interrogation room, after handing in his letter of resignation from the Cartel, he comes across a poster he had earlier made which read: 'WAKE UP WITH THE COCOA COMPLEXION'. This message he reduces to a revolutionary one: 'WAKE UP'.

The confrontation between the forces of oppression and exploitation and the forces of freedom and justice is growing. While Ofeyi's idea is beginning to put forth buds, the repressive measures of the purse and the gun are also becoming more open.

The meaning of 'Tentacles' is explained at the beginning of 'Tentacles VI'. The idea which had begun as Aiyéró communalism and had been translated by Ofeyi into something of a coherent philosophy with greater national significance is beginning to have off-shoots or 'tentacles'. Now the men of Aiyéró are penetrating into different parts of the country. Cross-river has been penetrated and the Shage Dam Project launched. On the other hand, the Cartel has 'at last identified its tormentors and organized a return harassment' (p. 86). With its 'long tentacles' (p. 86) and its alliance with the forces of repression and exploitation, the military regime, the Jeku and the Mining Trust, the Cartel is now determined to launch a ruthless campaign of re-assertion against its opponents. This means, among other things, the extermination of all foreigners to Cross-river, the foreigners being mainly the people of Aiyéró. 'I want a clean sweep of Cross-river', declares Zaki Amuri. The campaign also means, much to Ofeyi's dismay, the corruption of the minds of those under the sway of the pillars of the Cartel: 'The crime of Batoki and his vulgar noisy circle became even more heinous, acquiring dimension in its deliberate corruption of susceptible minds, creating mindless captive loyalties from dependants by blood or by inducements' (p. 146). The oppressed people decide to return the activities of the Cartel with violence. The dentist's answer to all this is that there should be a united front against the forces of oppression. The people's violence should be directed into a form of selective assassination of the key figures in the Cartel. After much debate within himself and after much persuasion from the dentist, Ofeyi comes to an acceptance of the necessity for violence in support of the oppressed masses.

'Harvest' represents the darkest hour for the lovers of life, freedom, justice and peace. Iriyise who is, as we shall see, a symbol of Ofeyi's philosophy, has been captured; the Shage Dam where Ofeyi's people had destroyed tribalism and regionalism creating 'new affinities, working-class kinships as opposed to the tribal' is destroyed (p. 170), Zaki Amuri's engineered carnage of foreigners in Cross-river spills over into outlying villages. Abominable crimes are committed: Sunday worshippers are trapped, burnt and massacred in a church, turning the Sunday worship into a Sunday sacrifice; the mortuary in the hospital where Chalil Ramath works is turned into a cold storage for storing butchered and outraged human bodies ... Horror past the description of horror.

For the forces of progress this is a dark hour. The forces of oppression have resorted to brutality of a bestial and inhuman nature. For the forces of oppression the massacres, the destruction of progressive projects, the capture of Iriyise are a harvest, a product of a well-planned course of action. There is a dialectical relationship between the growth of the progressive idea and the growth of brutality and human slaughter. The more developed Ofeyi's scheme is, the more horrors are wrought by the Cartel and its associates. It is a well-known fact that the more determined the oppressed people become in resisting exploitation and oppression, the more ruthless the oppressors become. In Soyinka's book the antagonism between the two forces finally leads to a hideous form of lawlessness which sweeps the whole country. It is this lawlessness which is symbolized by the title of the book, *Season of Anomy*.

In the general murder and destruction which sweeps the land, Ofeyi's vision suffers a severe blow and in fact appears to have been destroyed. But the forces of progress are more determined than ever to fight for justice and human freedom. The meeting between Ofeyi, Zacchus, Ahime and the Dentist, and their alliance with the Ramath family, are both symbolic of the coming together and mobilization of the forces of liberation into a united front. Putting aside the obvious fact that their struggle is meant to continue beyond what the book tells us, we can say that the culmination of their concerted action is the freeing of Iriyise from Temoko. But it is not only Iriyise who is freed here. In the final chapter of the book, we begin to see Ofeyi's revolutionary intellectualism bearing positive fruit in relation to the whole struggle. The quest for Iriyise results in the liberation of the instruments of oppression — those slaves who are used by their masters to enslave others. Through Ofeyi's influence Suberu's eyes are opened after twenty years of blind slavery, his mind is liberated and he decides to go with the liberators of Iriyise. As they leave the gates, other men join them, apparently from among the guards and other instruments of oppression in Temoko. They fall in with the forces of freedom, their minds liberated from a slave mentality which had bound them and others to the will of their enslaving masters.

The success of the plan depends partly on the co-operation of Chalil and Zaccheus, but ultimately on Demakin's organization and strategy. Here we see Ofeyi's mission and that of the Dentist merging. The purposeful assassin and the theoretical revolutionary ultimately meet in a moment of revolutionary action, and the contradictions between their approaches are resolved. In the final analysis it can be said that in a revolution each individual should play the part which best suits him. As long as the goals are the same, as long as the aim is the same, the different roles played by different people will complement each other and will eventually merge in the act of liberating man, in that supreme moment when the man of ideas ceases to be a mere thinker and becomes positively involved in the process of liberating those who are downtrodden. The act of freeing the enslaved and the act of removing the enslaver are only two sides of the same coin.

In freeing Iriyise and the guardians of the Temoko prison Ofeyi and Demakin have become 'Spores'; each is a seed that has developed to bear fruit, a single cell that has the capacity to grow and multiply.

Our study of symbolism in *Season of Anomy* cannot be complete without reference to Iriyise, who is not just a character but also a symbol. Her significance as a symbol is demonstrated in the cocoa pod dance at Shage where, as a pod, she lay hidden in the darkness of the soil, with 'no sensation except one of being buried alive', yearning for light, followed by a moment of rising slowly through the soil, 'light coming at last through the air holes' (p. 40). The significance of the dance comes out towards the end of the book when Iriyise is in a coma, almost dead. It is then that Suberu shows Ofeyi one of the earliest posters of Iriyise where she was depicted emerging from a pod: 'Iriyise was emerging from a neatly cracked golden egg-shape that represented the pod.' Suberu's association of the poster and the prostrate Iriyise is striking: 'The woman's condition was like that egg and Ofeyi must wait, patiently, for her emergence' (p. 314). The correctness of Suberu's interpretation is vindicated by the last sentence of the novel: 'In the forests, life began to stir.' In other words Iriyise began to come round, recovering from her deep coma.

But taken in the context of the theme of the book, the pod and the life go beyond the life of Iriyise as a character. Iriyise is not simply Ofeyi's girlfriend; she is a personification of Ofeyi's idea. The quest for Iriyise goes beyond the finding of Iriyise; it is a quest for an idea. It represents, among other things, Ofeyi's final decision to embrace the turbulence of violence as opposed to the artificial peace of passivity. This is clearly symbolized by Ofeyi's relationship with both Iriyise and Taiila. Taiila is the symbol of passive peace. She combines two principles of peace — her oriental background which can be associated with serenity and contemplation, and her admiration for the contemplative and peaceful life of Christian nuns. On the contrary, the search for Iriyise is a tumultuous search, requiring the searcher to take the most dangerous of risks. Ofeyi is at one time caught between these two apparently contradictory principles. At the moment of his reunion with Taiila he finds himself making comparisons between 'the infectious calm and the turbulent quest which would go beyond even the finding of Iriyise' (p. 240). Iriyise and Taiila can thus be seen to represent the contradictions in Ofeyi's personality — his natural inclination to non-violence on the one hand, and his eventual but painful acceptance of the necessity of violence on the other.

The search for Iriyise goes beyond the search of a woman for her own sake. This comes out clearly in the way Ofeyi answers Demakin when the latter asks: 'Tell me, why is it important? I mean, you have taken the most suicidal pains over this, we know that.' To this Ofeyi replies: 'Each person does what he is best at, remember?' And he goes on: '...I'm sure every man feels the need to seize for himself the enormity of what is happening, of the time in which it is happening. Perhaps deep down I realise that the search would immerse me in the meaning of the event, lead me to a new understanding of history' (p. 218).

Thus for Ofeyi the search leads to a greater understanding of the dynamics of history. Even the guerilla himself, Demakin, comes to a recognition of the necessity for relating the search for Iriyise to the revolutionary course of positively eliminating the chief exploiters of the people. His concept of the role of Iriyise is a radical and revolutionary one and is couched in some of the most powerful words in the book:

'But we must acknowledge the fact — pimps, whores, thieves, and a thousand other felons are the familiar vanguard of the army of

change. When the moment arrives a woman like Iriyise becomes
for them a Chantal, a Deborah, torch and standard-bearer, super-
mistress of universal insurgence. To abandon such a potential
weapon in any struggle is to admit to a lack of foresight. Or
imagination'.   (p. 219)

Texture and Readability

Soyinka's language is frequently difficult to understand. The difficulty is
largely the result of the density of texture and the abstract nature of the
language. Soyinka is found of the unusual word or expression and will
not just describe events without relating them to some abstract idea,
some concept that requires him to go beyond the mere narration of
events. The result of this is that his novel demands much concentration
and much puzzling out of meanings of words and expressions on the part
of the reader. This is apparent in the very first paragraph of the novel:

> A quaint anomaly, had long governed and policed itself, was so
> singly-knit that it obtained a tax assessment for the whole
> populace and paid it before the departure of the pith-helmeted
> assessor, in cash, held all property in common, literally, to the last
> scrap of thread on the clothing of each citizen — such an
> anachronism gave much patronizing amusement to the
> cosmopolitan sentiment of a profit-hungry society. A definitive
> guffaw from the radical centres of debate headed by Ilosa,
> dismissed Aiyéró as the prime example of unscientific
> communalism, primitive and embarrassingly sentimental ... Until
> its rediscovery at the time of the census ... the tourists swamped
> Aiyéró, then the sociologists armed with erudite irrelevances. Even
> the Corporation, intent on its ever-expanding cocoa drive took
> note of a new market for cocoa-bix and cocoa-wix. Ofeyi, the
> promotions man took his team down to Aiyéró.   (p. 2)

The reader will note the following expressions which are either unusual
or difficult to ascribe meanings to: 'gave much patronising amusement to
the cosmopolitan sentiment', 'a definitive guffaw', 'the radical centres of
debate', 'cocoa-bix', 'cocoa-wix'. It is not only the unusual word or
expression that is the source of obscurity here, but also the structure of
some sentences and the author's withdrawal of information when it is
required. The first sentence, for instance, is fairly involved and in it the
author mentions something without making it sufficiently clear to the
reader what he is talking about: 'A quaint anomaly, had long governed
and policed itself...' The reader is bound to be a little puzzled — what is
this 'quaint anomaly'? Why a comma after 'anomaly'? It is a paragraph
that is written with enthusiasm, but the enthusiastic tone is not matched
by clarity. The reader is being introduced to Aiyéró and its socialistic

ideals, but his mind is taxed before he can see clearly — if at all — what the author is getting at. It is not just semantic clarity that the reader expects, but he should be persuaded to read on.

Sometimes descriptions which are intended to affect the reader simply fail to bring out a clear picture. Here is a passage describing part of the ceremony performed by the people Aiyéró in honour of a dead Custodian of the Grain:

> The guilds approached, danced, retreated, leaving sinuous waves between the corpse and fourteen noble bulls penned before the alcove, one for each of the thirteen prior departed founding elders of the town. They were proud-horned, rich-humped, their brilliant ivory torsos rippled in the sun. Among them leapt the acrobats, in violent cartwheels, the female stilt-dancers bestrode them writhing suggestively above the humps, stooping low till their raffia skirts just covered the humps, only to twist away and leap over the herd looking back with mock-rebuke at the large watery eyes. The swirl of loincloths and daubed ochre, chalk and indigo turned the pen fluid, as if the enclosure were one vast churn of milk ...   (p. 14)

This, surely, is meant to be a vivid description of the dance. The lively rhythm of the language bears witness to this, so do such expressions as 'their brilliant ivory torsos rippled in the sun' which, no doubt, are meant to create a vivid picture in the reader's mind. But precisely what is going on here remains hazy. The reader to whom the ceremony is not familiar cannot picture clearly what is going on without a great deal of effort, and neither is he so impressed by the linguistic dexterity that he can ignore the obscurity.

The writer's technique of indirect statement or withholding information where the reader needs it merits further comment. It often occurs in conversational passages where we are given the impression that the interlocutors understand one another, whereas the reader is puzzled. The following is one example out of many that could be quoted:

> 'Have you seen this Sir? It was stuck right against the pillars of your driveway. One on each side.' The Chairman examined it, raced his mind to uncover the message before his analyst identified it for him ... 'After that loud-mouthed Jeku leader who boasted he would have his golden slice of the national cake.'
> 'Yes, yes I can tell that is the meaning. What I want to know is how it got stuck outside my gates. I have two of my own watchmen and both the police and the army are here in force. As you know we are expecting ...'
> 'Oh yes I heard that. Is it true?'
> 'Yes indeed it is. How embarrassing if he had had this to welcome him to the party.'   (pp. 34–5)

Of course the reader can understand that Ofeyi and his colleagues are launching a campaign against the officials of the Cartel by satirizing them on posters, but there is much that is not revealed here. The Chairman says: 'As you know we are expecting . . .', and IQ answers: 'Oh yes I heard that. Is it true?' There is no doubt here that the interlocutors understand one another, but their cryptic statements do not give sufficient information to the reader as to what they are talking about.

The withholding of information is not restricted to conversational passages. Even in his narrative the writer often refuses to be explicit, preferring to bring out his meaning through a process of indirect reference. This is true, for example, of the passage where he relates the story of the massacre of worshippers in a church. We are not told directly here that the people of Cross-river who carried out the heinous and horrifying act of trapping people in a church and setting the building on fire were Moslems. The reader has to infer this by interpreting the following sentences:

> It seemed at first a normal Sunday morning in the strangers' district, inhabited mostly by 'pagans' and Christians, all aliens to Cross-river.   (p. 196)
> They moved like ghosts . . . silent and clothed in the familiar dusty travesty of white robes.   (p' 197)
> It was evident that they were no Sunday worshippers.   (p. 197)

The reader who knows that Nigeria has a large Moslem population can only deduce from this that the people who wore 'white robes' and were not 'Sunday worshippers' were Moslems and that, accordingly, the population of Cross-river was a Moslem population.

Another, and perhaps a justifiable source of difficulty in Soyinka, is his attempt to penetrate into the depth of man's mind, into the depth of man's psyche by trying to probe into thinking processes and states of mind in a much more than superficial manner. His characters are capable of thinking deep thoughts. This is particularly true of Ofeyi whose imagination leaps into the unknown and seeks to probe into the whys and wherefores of things. Soyinka is an omniscient narrator and he attempts to record for the reader Ofeyi's thinking processes in a genuine manner, and this inevitably results in an abstract and difficult style. Here, for instance, is an extract showing Ofeyi's attempts to regain complete consciousness after being hit by Suberu.

> I am . . . trying to . . . break through . . . Surely some such phrase, some such message must be uppermost in her mind. There would be a strain exerted against the present tyrannical hold. She must be conscious of my presence here! Leaden arms perhaps, a sensation of slow congealment, a memory left on the shore of consciousness among discarded clothing, a slowing pulse . . . even so there must be the invisible near-titanic strain against the gluttonous maul, a fight to free the mind from its fly-paper trap of silence. If a marriage of

feelers could be effected by one magic moment, by a simultaneous
evocation of the many thoughts they had shared ... he tried to
concentrate on his actions which were one with what she
symbolized. He stressed his mind with the effort of concentration.
But she lay still.   (pp. 307–8)

The language here is abstract and obscure. But here obscurity is
justified, for it is balanced by a strenuous reaching into the maze of one
man's mind, the mind of a man who is anxious to communicate with a
beloved one who has been reduced to a state of lifelessness in terms of
both physical and mental powers. The intensity of Ofeyi's concentration
is reflected in the tautness of language. Ofeyi is struggling against the
tyrannical hold of death, hoping against hope to have some kind of
communication, some contact with the mind of Iriyise who is the very
symbol of his idea of purposeful action in a profit-hungry and ruthlessly
murderous society: 'He tried to concentrate on his actions which were
one with what she symbolized.[1] Apparently, after long hours of
unconsciousness he is still not very clear about what is happening, but
through sheer concentration and active thinking he is bringing himself
round to a full understanding of the present. Thus in his mental effort
Ofeyi is struggling to accomplish two things: on the one hand he
struggles to effect a state of consciousness in Iriyise, to stir her to her own
consciousness through his own deep thinking; on the other hand he tries
to regain complete consciousness, to possess a full understanding of his
own present predicament. It can also be said that regaining his own
consciousness is one and the same thing as regaining Iriyise, for Iriyise is
on one level a personification of his imagination. Soyinka manages to
bring out these complicated meanings through his use of language.

There is also a poetic quality here, evident not only in the density of the
language, but also in the imagery of expressions such as the following: 'a
memory left on the shore of consciousness among discarded clothing', 'if
a marriage of feelers could be effected by one magic moment', 'probing
with a million antennae', 'sieving out distracting atmospherics'. In these
expressions Soyinka attempts to create a psychological picture of the
cells of the brain, in order to give substance to mental states and to
thinking processes.

As is to be expected from a practising poet, Soyinka's language in
Season of Anomy is allusive, metaphorical and dense. The allusiveness of
the language is evident in the writer's use of myths and literary
references. He borrows liberally from the world's myths, from the Bible
and from English literature. There are references to Anubis who belongs
to Ancient Egyptian Mythology (p. 159), to Rana, who is probably a
Scandinavian goddess (p. 168), to Tarzan who, in Soyinka's own words,
was 'the ultimate primate of colonial fantasies' (p. 168). There are
numerous references to the Bible. There is, for instance, a reference to
Herod's massacre of the Innocent Children (p. 221), an incident which

finds a parallel in the Cartel's massacre of innocent workers; there is a reference to the Genesis story of the tree of life (p. 212); Ofeyi is at least twice referred to as the prodigal son (pp. 22 and 178), and so on. As for literary references, Soyinka draws on Shakespeare, Eliot, Yeats and others. Batoki is 'more sinned against than sinning' (p. 183), a line which comes straight from *King Lear*. As Ofeyi regains consciousness he finds himself quoting Yeats' poem, 'Long-Legged Fly': 'like a long-legged fly upon the stream — her mind moves upon the silence' (p. 307). At one time he is reminded of Eliot's famous line 'Fear death by water' which appears in *The Waste Land* (p. 105).

Perhaps the subtlest and most elusive example of allusion is one which runs through the entire length of the novel. This is the indirect reference to the story of Orpheus and his beloved Eurydice which occurs in Greek mythology. Just as Orpheus went to Hades, the underworld, in search of his dead wife Eurydice, Ofeyi descends into what Demakin the Dentist refers to as 'the bowels of Temoko' in a state of unconsciousness (or 'death') and only recovers when the liberation team is away in the forests. The restoration of Iriyise to the outside world and to life parallels Orpheus' attempts to bring Eurydice back to the land of the living. The correctness of this interpretation is borne out by the way Soyinka subtly refers to Cerberus in the character Suberu. In Greek mythology the job of Cerberus, the watchdog of Hades, is to keep the living from entering and the dead from leaving. Suberu is at least twice referred to as a 'dog' (pp. 290 and 316) and is indeed the watchdog of Temoko. In the story of the twelve labours of Hercules, Hercules' final labour is to bring Cerberus back from Hades. By taking Iriyise out of the darkness of Temoko and freeing Suberu from his slavery in the same place, Ofeyi has accomplished a truly Herculean task. It is most probable therefore that the names Ofeyi, Iriyise and Suberu have their origin in Greek mythology and are Africanized versions of Orpheus, Eurydice and Cerberus.

Further evidence of the poetic quality of Soyinka's style can be found in those satirical songs which Ofeyi composes for Zaccheus' band, for example:

> They milked the cocoa-tree in a mass operation.
> They drained the nectar, peeled the gold.
> The trees were bled prematurely old.
> Nor green nor gold remained for the next generation.   (p. 35)

The cocoa-tree is a symbol of the wealth of a nation which is exploited and destroyed by selfish monopoly capitalists like the members of the Cartel. Soyinka goes in for the unusual word even in these songs. In the first three verses the following words occur: 'ambrosia', 'elixir', 'amnesia' (p. 32).

Sometimes the language is poetic in rhythm, sound and movement and is capable of appealing to the reader, even if semantic clarity is vague. Consider the choice of words and the rich imagery of the following passage:

> Those roadside queens of the petty trade, ethereal in the morning light before the earthy transformation for their confrontation with bargaining humanity! They moved like wraiths through alleyways. Even burdened with the day's merchandise they are creatures of another world, their plump forms made even more shapeless by wads of wrappers and a money-belt securely round the waist. They leave the home with a softness extracted even from the key turning in the lock, from the two halves of a window married into place with a sleight of hand, a mere shush in the growing twilight; a final tug at the multitudinous folds and sash then footsteps fading into distance to minister to the needs of strangers ... and live, palpitating silence that follows their departure, a hive falling back into a last recoil before it joins the common frenzy in glare of daylight.   (p. 66)

Saying that such a passage appeals to the reader does not mean that it is not difficult. Here and in the other extracts quoted the reader is taxed and his reading speed slowed down. Soyinka compels the serious reader to have a dictionary by his side, and often to go over what he has read in order not to lose the thread of the story.

The early chapters of the book are particularly inhibiting. But the book becomes more and more absorbing, and by the end of 'Buds IV' the story has begun to capture the reader's interest. Ofeyi has taken a serious step in his attempts to undermine the Cartel, and his relationship with Iriyise is now of great significance to the reader. In later chapters of the novel events gather momentum, and the compelling power of the novel increases as the story of the horrors meted out to the people of Aiyéró by the Cartel and its tribalistic agents unfolds before us. In these later chapters the language is still abstract, but Soyinka is now able to hold the reader by the hand and lead him gently through the twists and turns of the plot. Many of the effective passages are about the savage killings and mutilations which take place in the book, acts which reduce the life of man to the level of rabid dogs. This ugly side of human nature is successfully symbolized by the dream which Ofeyi dreams before he and Zaccheus meet a strange group of killers on their way to Cross-river:

> Cramped half-asleep between the bed and wall he watched the thousands and thousands of slavering bare-fanged creatures emerge out of the corner of the floor and rush him ... Miraculously he found that his teeth were no longer human, that his jowls dribbled the dirty-ash, crimson-blotched spittle of a recent bestial banquet. His neck grew warm at the back as hairs rose on them in defiance, and, most wonderful of all, the sound that came from his throat was a perfect howl, fiercer than their prey-scenting wail.   (pp. 159–60)

The dream is a symbol of man's transformation into a jackal, a beast that takes pleasure in the ugly mutilations of the human body. It is, to quote Ofeyi's words in the dream, 'the eighth plague that the Judaic sorcerer had omitted to include — the plague of rabid dogs'. Significantly enough, the dream occurs shortly before one of the most horrifying incidents in the whole book. The cruelty and inhumanity of the so-called hunters whom Ofeyi and Zaccheus meet can only be portrayed in Soyinka's own words:

> Then someone unsheathed a dagger, placed it in his hand. It rose, glinted briefly in the sun and the old man stooped and drew it across the throat of the prostrate figure.
>
> His hand moved again, this time down the body, the knife-tip drew a swift, practised circle on the crotch and his other hand held up the victim's genitals. He passed it to one of the many eager hands which also uselessly held open a jaw that had opened wide to thrust out pain. Into that mouth they stuffed his penis with the testicles. Then they all stepped back and looked on the transformation they had wrought.   (p. 164)

Humans have indeed turned into rabid dogs. Even an animal deserves respect from man. One does not look at a dying dog with indifference: one is moved to compassion or pity; but not these human jackals. They are so insensitive that they take pleasure in committing acts that cry out to heaven in protest against the total lack of respect for the sanctity of the human body. These are shocking acts shockingly presented. The passage quoted here is only one of many told in a similar vein.

Through the dramatic and graphic language of such passages, Soyinka does not only evoke a sense of horror. He also arouses feelings of pity in the reader, pity for suffering humanity. A supreme example of pity is Soyinka's handling of the small community of Christians who had to bury themselves in the belly of a dark church, forced to live in hiding like the Christians of the first century who hid in catacombs, afraid of their Roman persecutors. The group's life becomes a life of prayer and fear. They are afraid of the savage killings of the Cartel and its hungry wolves, but their condition is such that they cannot escape death even here where they sing 'the Lord is my Shepherd, I shall not want'. Here is an extract describing the effect of a death among them:

> Knowledge of death filtered through the crypt, a chilly current through air that had only begun to warm up. The shadowy inmates underwent changes of infinite subtleties, drawing together even more, purging individual fears in the font of shared loss. Prayers rose in hushed voices from one corner to the other, a mother embraced her children in a sudden spasm of love, hugged them until they hurt. Her tears fell in mourning for the unknown one, death spread its cold tentacles through the festering gloom but

it bred no fear in the breasts of any. They had seen too
much. (p. 270)

Soyinka strikes a very human note here. The reader is moved to pity; he
is reminded of the tragic aspects of human existence. Because of greed
and selfish interests, man is compelled to reduce fellow man's life to a
state of utter misery and insecurity.

We should of course note that there is no attempt on the part of the
novelist to be merely melodramatic. Soyinka's description of horrors
and tragic scenes is extremely controlled. Sometimes he writes with some
kind of detached objectivity, as in the passage referred to above
describing the atrocities of the hunters, and yet the impact of the
language on the reader is powerful and satisfying.

Character and Language

Soyinka draws his main characters from diverse backgrounds. Ahime is
an old man, the leader of the people of Aiyéró. At times he appears
almost unreal: an old man in a traditional but ideologically progressive
African society, he is familiar with the idea of a Utopia (recalling Thomas
More's book) and with the writings of Mao. His conversations with
Ofeyi at the beginning of the book are marked by a level of sophistication
which, together with the picture of a well-read man which Soyinka
presents, leads the reader into asking: can this man exist in real life, given
the context in which he is portrayed? Soyinka refrains from giving us
sufficient information to enable us to adopt a definitive position. Ofeyi
and Demakin the Dentist are not indigenous to Aiyéró, and both have
travelled abroad. We also have Zaccheus and Iriyise, whose educational
background is not very clear. At any rate they may not have gone
through the higher levels of formal education, but they have a general
education and are alert to the social evils of their society. Taiila, Doctor
Chalil Ramath and Mrs Ramath are from India. Chalil is also well
travelled — born in India he studied in Britain and Germany, practised
in Britain for two years, and is now in Africa. All these characters
eventually find themselves collaborating in one way or another — they
belong to one 'ideological' camp. On the other side we find the Chairman
of the Cartel, Zaki Amuri, the Batoki family and the official Ofeyi
encounters in his search for Iriyise. Lastly there are the Spyholes and
Aristos of Soyinka's world.

Soyinka's characters are thus not limited to one region or one social
class. The setting is clearly Africa, probably Nigeria, but it is not
precisely described and not specified. The events could take place
anywhere where dictatorship, lawlessness and ruthless exploitation of
the type adumbrated in the novel prevail.

The author makes no attempt to Africanize the English language. In
fact he seems at times to be appealing mainly to a western readership, or

to both Europeans and Africans who have become western-oriented in their language and culture — this is the *effect* of his handling of his material, whether or not it is his intention.

I have already referred to his allusions to Shakespeare, Yeats and the Bible. The most striking example of Soyinka's appeal to a western-oriented readership is in his description of the Brigadier who unveils the statue of St George at the Cartel Chairman's party:

> The Brigadier bowed, took the scissors, took her hand and implanted a kiss upon it to thunderous applause and delight. He was a resplendent figure the Brigadier, groomed it seemed from a nineteenth-century Venetian court — appropriately, it had to be conceded, when the dust-sheet fell away and the glory of Italian marble was revealed to the benighted audience. Only the Chairman's running commentary jarred from time to time the viewers' contemplation of a Florentine moment in the heart of the festering continent.   (p. 44)

The scene reads almost like one from a Victorian or nineteenth century novel, showing British admiration for Italian art, culture and etiquette. The writer may of course have intended to satirize the glorification of European values in Africa. The key to this interpretation is in the last sentence where the contemplation of a Florentine moment (presumably referring to the art and beauty of Florence) is contrasted with 'the heart of the festering continent': Africa, a continent festering with moral depravity and disregard for human freedom and social justice, where the purse and the gun have made an unholy alliance to exploit and oppress the broad masses of the people. The satire continues into the second paragraph. Surely there is mockery in the hilarious tone of the following sentences:

> At the horse's feet writhed a monstrous dragon, scales of silver, tongue of bronze, fiery, fire-flashing eyes of onyx. It was transfixed by a ponderous silver spear and pounded by steel hooves of the noble steed.   (p. 44).

But it is not very clear whether Soyinka means to criticize the importation of European values, here celebrated not only in the British national symbol of St George and the dragon, but also in the vocabulary which portrays the British concept of nobility — 'noble plinth', 'armoured knight', and 'the noble steed'. It can equally be argued that he is simply appealing to a European or western-oriented readership — hence the reference to Italian culture, to Hannibal, Alexander and Boadicea. In fact this chapter is rather confusing, as it is not made clear whether some of the chief participants — Spyhole, the Brigadier and the host himself — are Africans or Europeans. The use of European names such as Spyhole, Zaccheus and Aristo for African characters adds to this confusion.

In their behaviour and language, some of Soyinka's characters are thoroughly European. This is especially true of Spyhole, the jovial journalist, of Zaccheus and, perhaps most important of all, the Chairman of the Cartel Corporation. The Chairman's address during the opening of his new fountain is typical of an Englishman in similar circumstances. Here is an extract from the speech:

> 'Ladies and Gentlemen, Distinguished visitors' — he bowed and bowed to unending cheers — 'Ladies and Gentlemen, the bar is still open, more dancing to our famous Zaccheus and his Cocoa Beans orchestra. And ... please attention please, attention Ladies and Gentlemen ... I think we are even fortunate enough to be able to promise, later, a personal appearance of none other than our Cocoa Princess, in one of her famous presentations, the title of which I'm afraid is being kept secret till the actual moment.'
> (p. 45)

Earlier on he addresses his audience as 'Ladies and Gentlemen, Distinguished Guests ...'

Of course it would be naive to maintain that it is only English or British people who are likely to speak in this way. As a result of the penetration of colonial culture in Africa, involving patterns of linguistic behaviour and etiquette as well as notions of refinement and civilization, African rulers and the intelligentsia have readily adopted European ways of speaking and European mannerisms in public behaviour.

Spyhole, Zaccheus and Mama Biye are among the few characters with a distinctive idiolect. Ofeyi's language is, of course, characterized by frequent flights of the imagination in moments of silent thought, but his conversational speech is not significantly different from that of Chalil or even Ahime. Spyhole does not say much. We learn about his idiolect as much from what the Chairman of the Cartel and the author say about him as we learn from his own speech. His style of speaking is lively and in his newspaper columns he is just as lively and at times downright bawdy. He is forthright in his denunciation of the European imported practice of beauty contests: ' "I still insist" he shrieked, "why must we ape this white charade!" ' He describes such contests as 'travesties of black womanhood' (p. 61). Referring to his admiration for Iriyise, the author says of him:

> 'His columns, witty and sensational, banal but sensational, predictable but sensational first and last wrote the sentences that founded the myth.'   (p. 62)

The longest conversation Spyhole holds with anybody occurs in 'Buds III' when he meets Zaccheus at the Cartel Chairman's party:

> 'Spyhole!'
> 'Zaccheus man how's it going?'

'B-sharp dead-on.'
'Any tips?'
'Deadwood.'
'Nobody got slapped yet?'
'Too much gold fluff man. You won't see a wig pulled tonight.'
'I thought not. Corruscated scene of starch.'
'And Madames and madamns and damnacadamns off their
  normal beat. All on their best behaviour.'
'Ah well. You've got the vantage point up there. If you see
  anything...'
'Sure I'll signal. So long Spy.'   (p. 37)

Spyhole and Zaccheus are evidently two of a kind. This colloquial and
informal style is typical of Zaccheus. He has a jovial and lively manner of
talking and could pass for a working-class mother-tongue speaker of
English or, specifically, for a black American. In fact he reminds one of
the great black American jazz star, the late Louis Armstrong. Here is a
conversation between him and Ofeyi, whose words open the
conversation:

'Are you going to play the damned thing?'
'Coming boss coming. Man, you and Celestial are real touchy
this morning.'
He blew softly, lingering over each phrase and caressing the
notes...
'I don't know why I let Celestial give me that scare. There is no
thorn in it man, not with a melody like that. Just ambrosia man,
nectar and ambrosia like you name it in that other number.'
Ofeyi laughed. 'You want me to change the words round.'
'What? Oh no. That's mere words and spikes — not that the tune
isn't sweet and seductive and all that. But this ...! Hey man, why
don't you just stay with us ...'   (p. 76)

Zaccheus' hilarious style of speaking makes him one of the most
memorable characters in the whole book.
   Mama Biye, Batoki's querulous wife, is notable for her powers of
speech. She is a shrew with a shrill voice, a shameless woman who knows
no limit in her wild vituperations against her husband and against her
daughter, Biye, of whom she is intensely jealous. Batoki is one of the four
pillars of the Cartel, but at home he is a humiliated man, a slave to the
constant barrage of a sharp-tongued wife. This creates an ironic
situation which makes it impossible for Ofeyi and the Dentist to attempt
assassinating Batoki — they pity him rather. Mama Biye is also the
character whose language seems to be closest to African idioms. In the
following passage she is railing at her husband:

'Gossip! Doesn't she bring her disease-ridden friends for you to
sleep with? Of course what else can one expect? There isn't a single

streak of honest dealing in the family of the Batokis, there never was. She has inherited your blood, no doubt about that! I thought I could close my eyes to the number of houses you bought outside to lodge your mistresses but I never thought my own daughter would bring those free-for-alls for my husband to sleep with, under my roof.'

'Keep your voice down if you must retail these stupid gossips . . .'

'It is hardly your fault of course,' she continued, raking him downwards again with contemptuous eyes. 'It is the fault of those who took pity on the bare neck of the vulture and lent him a shawl. They weren't to know he would forget a time when the cold winds froze the blood before it could even reach his head.'   (pp. 184–5)

These last words of Mama Biye are the closest to an African idiom in *Season of Anomy*. In the rest of the book the question whether Soyinka's characters are speaking in their native tongue becomes quite irrelevant. Soyinka uses Standard English, his characters speak English as though it is their mother tongue.

Conclusion

Soyinka's novel is stylistically difficult. It is not easy for the average reader to penetrate through the complexities of symbol and verbal structure which characterize the novel. These difficulties will prevent many readers from enjoying one of Soyinka's most important artistic creations to date, for *Season of Anomy* is not only a very accomplished novel, it also marks a significant turning point in Soyinka's profession as a writer. The theme of the novel is based on the dialectical relationship between exploitation and revolution, and Soyinka points to the inevitability of violence as a method of bringing about justice to the oppressed peoples of Africa. For thinking people like Ofeyi the prevailing social conditions present a serious challenge. But the challenge applies no less to Soyinka than it does to Ofeyi, for Soyinka is certainly becoming a militant writer. This was already apparent in his small book of poems, *Ogun Abibiman*, which hailed President Machel's announcement that the Mozambique nation had placed itself in a state of war against Rhodesia. This recent commitment on the part of Soyinka is clearly stated in his introduction to *Ch'Indaba*, a journal of which he is the editor. There he expresses the view that it is not in the nature of man to sit idly while political events 'roll over him':

It may be therefore that the battle is joined only on paper — nevertheless it is a battle and, whatever sense of futility may occasionally overwhelm those who wage it from a sense of identity with the victim as a human victim, not as an abstraction, the intensity of outrage cannot be lessened, nor the criminal leaders be allowed to retain the last word on the fate of peoples.[3]

Notes

1 See, for example, E. Jones, *The Writing of Wole Soyinka*, pp. 10–11.
2 *The Necessity of Art: A Marxist Approach*, p. 108.
3 *Ch' Indaba*, Vol. 3, No. 1, 1977, p. 5.

8 Ayi Kwei Armah — *Two Thousand Seasons*

▼▼▼▼▼▼▼▼▼▼▼▼▼▼▼▼▼▼▼▼▼▼▼▼▼▼▼▼▼▼▼

Introduction to Theme and Style

The first thing to note about this novel is the scale of the time span — literally two thousand seasons. This probably means one thousand years. The idea of two seasons in a year occurs on p. 6: 'Before Anoa's utterance then, our migrations were but an echo to the alternation of drought and rain.' And again: 'But why should we make an unending remembrance of drought and rain, the mere passage of seasons?' In the scheme of the novel time is measured in terms of these two basic seasons, the dry one and the wet one.

The next thing to note is the range of historical coverage. This entails an assertion of African values and a rejection of foreign values, foreign domination and foreign social systems. The assertion of African values involves, among other things, a yearning to return to the roots of African history, an assertion of the unity of the African peoples and of their common origin, and an attempt to bring about a noble and truly African society.

The unity of the African people is expressed in clear and uncompromising terms: 'That we the black people are one people we know. Destroyers will travel long distances in their minds and out to deny you this truth' (p. 3). Armah makes it clear that he is not writing about a selected group of Africans. Throughout the novel we see a community of black people struggling together against a common enemy. There is no specification of a particular geographical place, except that the events clearly take place on the African continent. There is no doubt that if Armah has in mind one geographical area as the original home of all the African peoples, that area is North Africa, including the area covered by ancient Egypt and the region now known as the Sahara Desert. It is this latter area which the destroyers from the desert — the Arabs — have made barren.

The most obvious example of Armah's attempt to assert the oneness of the African people is his use of names: the names of his characters come from all over Africa. There are West African names such as Inse, a Ghanaian name and the name of Armah's own son; Soyinka, a Yoruba name of Nigeria; and Kamara, a name which appears in *Sundiata*, the Mali epic. From East Africa we have Kamuzu, who reminds us of Dr Kamuzu Banda of Malawi, and there is a reference to Mzee (Kenyatta) on p. 172. From southern Africa there is Isanusi, a Zulu name; Azania, the African name for South Africa; Mofolo, a Sesotho name; and others. Armah evidently learned some of these names from his reading of African literature. Mofolo is the name of the celebrated Mosotho writer, Thomas Mofolo. Both Isanusi and Noliwe (Noliwa) are characters in Mofolo's *Chaka*. Isanusi is Chaka's doctor (in Armah Isanusi is a healer) and Noliwa is Dingiswayo's sister and Chaka's girl friend.

The common origin of the African people, 'the people of the way', is known to the *fundi*, the experts of the people's arts, the seers and the healers; Isanusi is a senior *fundi*. The common origin of the people is also taught to the young people who narrate the story, the young revolutionaries who have dedicated themselves to the rebuilding of Africa, the young militant combatants who look up to Isanusi, the healer, for ideological training. It is part of their initiation to learn about the origins of the people of the way:

> But this we learned then: that we came from drier places, wide open places where eyes can see across fields like seeing across seawater. Trees cut your vision, but they are few, solitary, almost strangers in the place. This place, our present home, is more abundant. The soil here is softer, the rain incomparably more generous ...   (p. 87)

This place where there are no trees to disturb one's vision, where the soil is hard and rain scarce, is North Africa, presumably Egypt, where in ancient times people depended on the waters of the Nile to irrigate their fields. The area may also include Africa's tropical savannas. In *Sundiata*, for instance, Mali is called 'the Bright Country, the savanna land'.[1]

The enemies of 'the people of the way' include two principal enemies — the ostentatious cripples from the desert, the Arabs, and the destroyers from the sea, the European colonialists. These two principal enemies create other enemies from among the people themselves, the zombis and askaris who are the willing instruments of the destroyers, and puppet rulers such as Kamuzu. Kings like Koranche, and their flatterers like Otumfur, have collaborated with the white men in enslaving African people and exploiting them and are therefore to be condemned as enemies of the people.

The foreign values which are rejected in the novel include Islam and Christianity, the white man's view of African history and the destroyers' exploitation of the African.

Both Islam and Christianity are regarded as instruments of cultural colonization which have led the African into forgetting 'the way' and into rejecting African values as he seeks to identify with the enemy. Thus one African Moslem is despised for taking an Arab name: 'He called himself after the predator's fashion, Abdallah, a name he said signified he was a slave — slave of a slave-owning god' (p. 36). In his rejection of the white man's Christianity Isanusi says: 'They say it will be reward enough when we have lost our way completely, lost even our names; when you will call your brother not Olu but John, not Kofi but Paul; and our sisters will no longer be Ama, Naita, Idawa and Ningome but creatures called Cecilia, Esther, Mary, Elizabeth and Christina' (p. 83).

The white man's view of African history will be referred to later in this section. Now a word about Armah's rejection of the exploitation of the African by the white destroyers from the sea. The rejection is most eloquently expressed in Isanusi's speech before his exile when he tells the people that the white man has five wishes: to rob their land of mineral resources; to kill all the animals roaming the land; to rob them of their land and to use them as a source of cheap labour; to take their people into slavery; to convert them to Christianity (pp. 82–3). This neatly summarizes Armah's view of what the European races have done to Africa since the slave trade.

The answer to the African problem is provided by the young revolutionaries, the utterers, the narrators of the tale who have dedicated themselves to 'the way'. Theirs is a strong determination to wage a liberation war against imperialism and neo-colonialism in the hope of establishing a truly independent society. They accept guerrilla warfare as a viable method of asserting African independence. This is in line with what Africa has come to regard as the only way of removing the last vestiges of colonialism in Africa — the armed struggle.

With this theme in view, we can now turn to a brief discussion of the writer's style. First, with regard to point of view, Armah uses a technique not used by any of the other authors discussed in this volume. The story is not told by one of the characters. Nor does it seem to be told by the author, who is apparently outside the story itself and appears only as a prophet in the Prologue. Even then Armah has distanced himself from his work in such a way that it is not clear whether it is the author who utters the Prologue or not. The narrator in *Two Thousand Seasons* is the collective voice of the young revolutionaries who have dedicated themselves to 'the way'. This is not immediately clear, but the evidence is at the end of Chapter 3 where the utterers say: 'It was in Koranche's time as king that the children of our age grew up. It was also in his time — disastrous time — that the white destroyers came from the sea' (p. 74).

Theirs then is a collective voice in the true tradition of African communalism where the community is more important than the individual. Accordingly the operative word is 'we'. 'I' hardly occurs. 'We' opens the first paragraph of the first chapter: 'We are not a people of yesterday' (p. 1). At times the repetition of 'we' is of obvious stylistic significance, as in the following passage:

> Remembrance has not escaped us. Trapped now in our smallest self, we, repositories of the remembrance of the way violated, we,

portion that sought the meaning of Anoa's utterance in full and found another home on this same land, we, fraction that crossed mountains, journeyed through forests, shook off destruction only to meet worse destruction, we, people of the fertile time before these schisms, we, life's people, people of the way, trapped now in our smallest self, that is our vocation: to find our larger, our healing self, we the black people.   (pp. 8–9)

In this short passage the word 'we' appears six times and determines the rhythm of the whole passage. Except in the last phrase, the word is followed by a pause in each unit and then by a long clause explaining an aspect of the history of the people of 'the way'. There is an interesting experiment with the device of parallelism here. Although the language is prose, it is highly patterned as in poetry. 'We' occurs in equivalent positions, at the beginning of each unit so that it constitutes the invariant part of the parallelism, and the rest of the unit the variant part.[2] This sentence is typical of Armah in *Two Thousand Seasons*: it is a long rhetorical periodic sentence preceded by a very short one. The long sentence is characterized by repetitions of key words and by balances and a flowing rhythm. It is a periodic sentence because it delays the expression of the writer's complete thought until the very end. The complete meaning emerges when we come to 'that is our vocation ...'.

A passage from the last chapter of the book will serve as another example. Here the young revolutionaries, the utterers, clarify their position on the question of the armed struggle which they have ultimately accepted as a viable method of destroying the white destroyers:

We do not utter praise of arms. The praise of arms is the praise of things, and what shall we call the soul crawling so low, soul so hollow it finds fulfilment in the praising of mere things? It is not things we praise in our utterance, not arms we praise but the living relationship itself of those united in the use of all things against the white sway of death, for creation's life. That is the beauty of the seers' vision, that alone is music to the hearers' ear. That is the sole utterance of utterers conscious of our way, the way. Whatever thing, whatever relationship, whatever consciousness takes us along paths closer to our way, whatever goes against the white destroyers' empire, that thing only is beautiful, that relationship only is truthful, that consciousness alone has satisfaction for the still living mind.   (pp. 205–6)

This is representative of some of Armah's best passages in the novel. As in the previous example, the opening sentence is a short simple sentence. The second sentence, partly a statement and partly a rhetorical question, is quite long. The argument of the utterers is presented in stages. The first sentence tells us that the revolutionaries do not praise arms. The second goes on to explain why they do not praise arms — they are mere things, a means to an end. The third sentence then tells us what is to be praised: 'the living relationship itself' of those united against the sway of death. Then the passage reaches its lyrical climax as the writer emphasizes in poetic language the beauty of the relationship he has described.

The well-placed repetition, the powerful rhythms, the skilful balancing of words, clauses and sentences, and the intensity of feeling: these are some of the qualities of this passage that account for its powerful effect. The reader will note how, in the second sentence, 'the praise of arms' is complemented and balanced by 'the praise of things', and how 'soul crawling so low' is complemented by 'soul so hollow'. Parallelism is exploited to the full. The poetry that results from the parallelism and from the rhythm of the language is best demonstrated by the last sentence where 'whatever' recurs four times, though each time followed by a different word from the one preceding: first it is followed by 'thing', then by 'relationship', then by 'consciousness', and lastly by the verb 'goes'. In the second part of the sentence 'what' is complemented by 'that' which occurs three times; followed first by 'thing', then by 'relationships' and then by 'consciousness' — thus balancing perfectly the order of words in the first part of the sentence. It is also significant to note that in the second part of the sentence each of the three nouns is given an attribute: that thing is 'beautiful', that relationship is 'truthful', that consciousness 'has satisfaction for the still living mind.'

Lastly it is important to note that there is a certain degree of seriousness and dignity here which makes it legitimate for us to describe the language as sublime (see the following section). We have noted the powerful rhythmical movement of the language and the intensity of feeling and thought that is evident in the passage. We should also note the solemn tone that results from the use of words which in the context of the novel have acquired a formal ring, words like 'utter', 'utterance', 'seer', 'the way'. Such elevation and intensity of thought and feeling is a characteristic feature of the whole novel. This is evident not only in the Prologue where the author–prophet makes a passionate appeal to the African race, to the prophets of Africa, to its thinkers and patriotic sons, but also in the opening paragraphs of the first chapter where the utterers are rejecting the European conception of African history:

> We are not a people of yesterday. Do they ask how many single seasons we have flowed from our beginnings till now? We shall point them to the proper beginning of their counting. On a clear night when the light of the moon has blighted the ancient woman and her seven children, on such a night tell them to go alone into the world. There, have them count first the one, then the seven, and after the seven all the other stars visible to their eyes alone.
>
> After that beginning they will be ready for the sand. Let them seek the sealine. They will not have to ponder where to start. Have

> them count the sand. Let them count it grain from single grain.
>   And after they have reached the end of that counting we shall not
> ask them to number the raindrops in the ocean. But with the
> wisdom of the aftermath have them ask us again how many
> seasons have flowed by since our people were unborn.   (p. 1)

The language here is mellow, it is incantatory, enchanting. It appeals to
the imagination and has the effect of carrying the mind far away. The
narrators are talking about the long history of the black peoples of
Africa, symbolized by the innumerable stars in the African sky, by the
uncountable sand on the African shores, and by the number of raindrops
in the ocean. Those who claim to know our history cannot count the
stars in the sky, the sand on the seashore, the raindrops in the ocean. By
the same token they cannot claim to know how many seasons have
passed since the beginning of our history. We should note that 'seven' is a
significant figure in the novel: it recurs a number of times and the seven
stars mentioned here seem to be guiding stars for 'the people of the way'.
In their epic march to their new home they watch the ancient woman and
the seven stars in order to get their bearings. The book itself is divided
into seven chapters. The figure seven also appears in *Sundiata* where
Sundiata is described as 'the seventh star, the seventh conqueror of the
earth'. His mother, Sogolon Kedjou, also called the Buffalo woman, is
surrounded by mystery. The ancient woman of Armah's novel is
reminiscent of Sogolon.

In its opening passages, therefore, the book rejects the white man's
view of African history, the view of those who claim that 'we are a people
of yesterday', that we have no history, or that our history begins with
colonialism. The utterers then go on to show how this 'mutilation' of our
history is part of the destruction of our people. These 'fragments', these
'shards' which 'they' bring are 'part of the wreckage of our people'. These
distortions are part of the enemy's attempt to deceive us and to take from
us what properly belongs to us. In this connection it is appropriate to cite
the example of Ancient Egypt, an African civilization, which Europeans
tend to take as part of their heritage. The distortions of African history
by Europeans, the dangers, the cruelty and ugliness of such distortions,
are effectively expressed in the following metaphor: 'It is their habit to
cut off fingers from the hand itself uprooted from its parent body, calling
each fallen piece a creature in itself, different from ears, eyes, noses, feet
and entrails, other individual creatures of their making' (pp. 1–2).

The passionate feeling behind Armah's language that runs through
the novel is best demonstrated in a passage from the Prologue. Here the
narrator takes upon himself the role of a prophet warning Africa against
its naive generosity, which can only lead to its own destruction:

> Woe the race, too generous in the giving of itself, that finds a road
> not of regeneration but a highway to its own extinction. Woe the

race, woe the spring. Woe the headwaters, woe the seers, the hearers, woe the utterers. Woe the flowing water, people hustling to our death.   (pp. xii–xiii)

'Woe' is a word which curses and shows anger — often righteous anger. It is also a word which shows utter grief, as in 'Woe is me!' A good example of how this word can express the speaker's righteous anger is in Chapter 23 of St Matthew's Gospel (verses 13 ff) where Jesus curses the scribes and pharisees for hypocrisy and for preaching what they do not practise. In Armah the word 'woe' is the expression of a prophet who is not only angry but also grief-stricken at the foolish generosity of Africa: a continent that warmly receives strangers who eventually destroy her original inhabitants, robbing them of their wealth, their culture and their independence. The skilful use of parallelism here is obvious: it depends on the repetition of the phrase 'woe the' which forms the invariant part of each relevant unit. The result is powerful rhythm and persuasive language.

Thus we can note that Armah's style is very expressive; it overtly shows the writer's feelings and attitudes towards his subject, and it shows a serious concern with diction, the choice of a special kind of word. It is forceful, persuasive and at times necessarily revolting. Since Armah's style depends on devices such as parallelism, repetition and imagery, his language may be described as poetic prose.

Epic Qualities

Two Thousand Seasons is a novel conceived on a grand scale. Although the basic argument presented in the book revolves around a time span of about a thousand years, the events described go even further back into the past of the black peoples of Africa. The novel therefore covers an indisputably long span of time and challenges black people to go back to the very roots of the African nation. At the same the novel looks forward to a victorious future when the African will be independent of the destroyers, having reasserted his own position, his own world view, his own culture. *Two Thousand Seasons* is to that extent a novel of epic proportions. Can we therefore describe it as an epic novel, a novel which is much more than an ordinary novel?

To answer this question we need to define the characteristic of an epic. First, let us cite some of the well-known epics of the world. From Italy there is Virgil's *Aeneid*, whose theme is that of a great hero destined to found a great city, one of the greatest centres of civilization, Ancient Rome; from Africa there is *Sundiata*, which relates the life and exploits of the great Sundiata the founder of the ancient Empire of Mali; from Britain there is Milton's *Paradise Lost*, which attempts to encompass the creation of the universe, the struggle between God and Satan and the Fall of Man, within the context of the Christian myth.

Here are some of the characteristics of an epic.

1.   An epic is usually a long narrative poem, showing skilful workmanship, recounting many episodes and giving unity and form to 'great masses of material'.[3]
2.   The epic has its roots in oral tradition and is regarded as an amalgam of myth, history and fiction.
3.   An epic is of strong national significance. The *Aeneid*, for instance, is a nationalistic epic *par excellence*, seeking to give a heroic account of the mission of the founder of Rome and to glorify Rome.
4.   The epic is written in an elevated style.
5.   Epics like *Paradise Lost* include such conventions as the invocation of the Muse, the participation of divine beings in the great events of the poem, war, verbal combat, the roll-call of leaders, the combination of sublimity and simplicity in style.

Two Thousand Seasons seems to fulfil many such criteria. Although it is a novel, it has many poetic qualities, rooted in the oral traditions of Africa. We have already established that it is a novel conceived on a grand scale. It is a long novel. It certainly covers 'great masses of material' and has a strong national significance for Africa.

It is the most outspoken novel to be written so far on the unity and common cause of the black peoples of Africa. Its theme is a very serious one and reflects the author's genuine desire to see Africa truly independent and free from outside interference and exploitation. Armah's passionate nationalism and his pan-Africanist spirit give rise to what may be called anti-racist racialism. The attitude of the author to Arabs and Europeans may be taken as an extremist one by some readers. The same may also be said of his views on Christianity and Islam.

On the question of Armah's nationalism it should be noted that when the novel ends, what was a purely African problem is transformed into a universal problem. There is recognition of the fact that it is not only Africans who have suffered from European imperialism: 'Their greed is far-flung, far beyond our land. Other lands have burned in their insatiate avarice, other peoples have died in the whiteness of their greed' (p. 205). This being the case, all the races which have been subjected to white imperialism and oppression will identify with one another, will stand together in their common struggle: 'each people of the way will find every other people of the way' (p. 205). Indeed the book ends with a passionate declaration of the universal nature of the struggle:

> Against this what a vision of creation yet unknown, higher, much more profound than all erstwhile creation! What a hearing of the confluence of all waters of life flowing to overwhelm the ashen desert's blight! What an utterance of the coming together of all the people of our way, the coming together of all people of the way!   (p. 206)

This is a forceful affirmation of the ultimate triumph of the people of the way against the white man's destruction. The hope is expressed in the excited tone and in the powerful symbolism embodying the author's vision of a triumphant future, particularly the image of the confluence of waters which will ultimately overcome the desert. Note that the emphasis is on 'all the waters of life' and 'all people of the way' — embracing all the oppressed peoples of the world who are struggling against injustice and the exploitation of man by man. Here we are reminded of Lenin calling on all the workers of the world to unite; of the goal of socialism which aims at ultimate victory for workers and peasants the world over; of the people of the Third World struggling together to defeat super power politics, capitalism and imperialism. In this respect *Two Thousand Seasons* is a modern epic which incorporates modern progressive thinking, for the most revolutionary sons of Africa believe that their revolution is not limited to Africa but is part of the universal struggle for freedom, independence and social justice.

Yet another feature which justifies calling the novel an epic is the style. There is no doubt that the style has many elements of sublimity, as defined in classical Europe. Longinus gives what he calls 'five sources of the grand style': first, 'the ability to form grand conceptions'; second, 'the stimulus of powerful and inspired emotion'; third, 'the proper formation of two types of figures, figures of thought and figures of speech'; fourth, 'the creation of a noble diction, which in its turn may be resolved into the choice of words, the use of imagery, and the elaboration of style'; and lastly, 'the total effect resulting from dignity and elevation'.[4]

Armah's style fulfils at least some of these conditions. There is no doubt that his style is conceptual — his language is an expression of grand ideas. Many passages in the book have the effect of challenging the reader to relate what he reads to intellectual ideas. This expression of grand conceptions is evident in the Prologue, in the first chapter and the last chapter, where ideas are expressed with an intensity of feeling and thought which captivates and elevates the mind. That Armah's style is capable of stimulating emotions is easily proved by reference to our discussion of Chapter 2. He has created noble diction: such careful choice of word and phrase, together with flowing rhythms and powerful imagery, combine to produce an incantatory style which enchants the reader. This, too, is particularly true of the Prologue, the first chapter and the last chapter. It is also in these chapters of the book that the sensitive reader most effectively experiences what Longinus calls 'the total effect resulting from dignity and elevation'. The author's style in these chapters is truly dignified and free from the rather disturbing language of the second chapter.

But in this novel sublimity is coupled with simplicity. It is a book which is quite easy to read. The following is a passage which is typically simple. Isanusi is explaining the exploitative nature of the mission of the white destroyers from the sea. There is none of the political jargon with which African leaders are bombarded nowadays. There is no attempt to use difficult words or to use words for the sake of their sound:

> 'Hear now the end. The white men wish us to destroy our mountains, leaving ourselves wastes of barren sand. The white men wish us to wipe out our animals, leaving ourselves carcases rotting into white skeletons. The white men want us to take human beings, our sisters and our sons, and turn them into labouring things. The white men want us to take human beings, our daughters and our brothers, and turn them into slaves. The white men want us to obliterate our remembrance of our way, the way, and in its place to follow their road, road of destruction, road of a stupid, childish god.'   (pp. 83–4)

Of course the degree of simplicity differs from one part of the novel to another. Some passages are only superficially simple. Much of the last chapter, for example, is allusive and requires the interpreter to know something about socialism, armed struggle, and the predicament of the Arabs and their relations with other races in the modern world. They are said to be 'willing instruments of worse predators than themselves, of destroyers even greedier' (p. 205). This is a reference to the Europeans or the Isarelis against whom the Arabs are struggling. Some of the symbols used are quite obscure and cannot permit a simple interpretation. There is the symbol of the ancient woman and her seven children in Chapter 1. In the fifth chapter we have a particularly beautiful but sophisticated symbol — the symbol of the river and the sea:

> Where the river met the sea its easy flow gave way to a wild turbulence. The seawater came in long, curling waves to a meeting with the darker water from the land. In both waters there was a forward motion, so at the place of their meeting there was no quiet mixing but a violent upward surge from clashing waves. A wall of water stretched unbroken the whole length of the river-mouth and beyond. Here in the moving, constant barrier formed from the meeting of the waters there was a tremendous beauty. At times the massive spray rose higher than any wawa tree.   (pp. 75–6)

I was struck so much by the beauty of the symbolism of this passage that I asked Mr Armah what the river and the sea stood for; his answer was that the river symbolizes the particular and the sea the universal. What is significant is the turbulence resulting from the confluence of the river and the sea. Does this symbolize the turbulence that results from the meeting of the particular and the universal? Is the writer perhaps suggesting that the black people are a particular race with its own particular way of life, and that as soon as its particularity is disturbed by coming into contact with the universal there is bound to be a violent clash? Whatever the case, this is a complex, sophisticated use of imagery.

There are other features which place the novel within the epic tradition, such as the use of the roll-call. But a more important claim for

Two Thousand Seasons is its synthesis of myth, fiction and history.

Armah does not, strictly speaking, recreate a myth that is ready-made and widely accepted, but he has created a myth for the African people. Much of the novel has no historical basis, being of Armah's own making. Such characters as Anoa, Ningome and Juma are probably fictitious and so are many of the events narrated. But the fiction is related to historical fact. It is historically true, for instance, that the peoples of Africa moved from more open lands and drier places to the thick forests and wet areas of the centre, the west and the south of the continent. It is historically true that Africa was invaded by Arabs and Europeans. It is a fact that Africans were taken into slavery by white people. This historical orientation is a source of strength for the novel. Those parts of the book which are closely related to the history of Africa are among the most convincing, while those parts where Armah distorts African history or the African tradition in order to promote his own ideology are sometimes not very convincing. Is it reasonable, for instance, to suggest that before African people were exiled from 'the way' they had no kings?

There is at least one respect, however, in which *Two Thousand Seasons* is very far removed from the traditional epic. In such epics gods are involved in human events and destiny, and are frequently a force that determines the course of men's lives. In *Sundiata*, for example, Sundiata the Great is destined to be the ruler of Mali and nothing will stand in his way, neither a handicapped childhood nor the jealousies of his enemies will stop him being the founder of a big empire. In *The Aeneid*, Aeneas the father of the Romans is destined to found the city of Rome, and such obstacles as falling in love with Dido, the queen of Egypt, must be overcome. In Armah's novel, gods play no role and destiny does not feature at all. This is a reflection of Armah's attitude towards the whole question of religion. It is sufficiently clear from his criticism of Christianity and Islam and from his total silence on the question of the 'people of the way's' religious beliefs that he sees no place for a god in the scheme of things. His thinking may not necessarily be that of historical Marxism but is certainly akin to it. Thus *Two Thousand Seasons* can be regarded as a modern epic in the sense that it is a reflection of the modern age which has denied the existence of God.

Armah's Use of Affective and Evocative Language

Armah's language can arouse feelings and emotions; it shows the writer's own feelings towards the object or person described. Armah uses words with strong affective connotations. The chapter which best demonstrates this aspect of his style is the second chapter, 'The Ostentatious Cripples', a chapter that is devoted to what the author considers to be the depravity of the Arabs. Arabs are here portrayed as highly sensual and incapable of resisting the physical appetites. To portray their debased pleasures, Armah chooses to describe a time of feasting after a Ramadan, the Muslim period of fasting. In this way he manages to give an absurd

picture of the Arabs' love of food, drugs and above all sex. The askaris,
those African zombis used by the destroyers to oppress the masses of the
people, are also portrayed as reflecting the pleasure-loving nature of
their masters, while black women are depicted as extremely generous.
The women send the following quantities of food to the askaris:

> a dozen dripping lamps freshly taken from their frying fat, spiced
> hollow yams, seven whole cows turned two days and nights over
> slow fires, with only the liver, heart, the kidneys, brains and thigh
> meat taken from each beast. Of drink the askaris received an even
> greater sufficiency, for a little was all that was needed to make the
> predators themselves stupid with happiness uncontainable.
> (p. 20)

The sensuousness of the askaris and their masters is reflected in such
expressions as 'a dozen *dripping* lambs', *'freshly* taken', 'frying fat', 'spiced
hollow yams', 'greater sufficiency'. The language here reflects the quality
of the food: the soft sounds of the words and the alliteration are as
appealing to the ear as the food itself is appealing to the taste.

   The absurdity of the Arabs' sensuousness, lust and greed is described
on the following page:

> Great was the pleasure of these lucky Arab predators as with
> extended tongue they vied to see who could with the greatest ease
> scoop out buttered dates stuck cunningly into the genitals of our
> women lined up for just this their pleasant competition. From the
> same fragrant vessels they preferred the eating of other delicious
> food: meatballs still warm off the fire, their heat making our women
> squirm with a sensuousness all the more inflammatory to the
> predators' desire. The dawa drug itself the predators licked
> lovingly from the youngest virgin genitals — licked with a furious
> appetite.   (p. 21)

The first of these sentences revolts the reader as it describes an absurd
form of sexual practice. In the second sentence the appetizing food and
the excitement with which the Arabs enjoy it is reflected in the sensuous
appeal of the language. Sex, eating and drug-taking are described in this
chapter as the most pleasurable things of the Arab, and it is these that
send Hussein, Faisal, Hassan and the other Arabs to their death. The
passage describing the revelry and death of Hussein is appealing and at
the same time shocks and revolts the reader. Note how the rhythm,
pauses and alliteration reflect the Arabs' excitement on this night of
nights:

> Hussein, twin brother of Hassan the Syphilitic. Hussein had long
> since given up the attempt to find a way for his phallus into any
> woman's genitals. His tongue was always his truest path-
> finder...   (p. 21)

Hussein is not manly; he is incapable of having normal sexual intercourse with a woman and thus resorts to the depraved practice of using his tongue and of eating dates which have been scooped out of a woman's private parts. In the course of this abominable act he gets dizzy and the women he is luxuriating with stab him to death. The end of Hussein's death is described with verbal expertise:

> That devout Muslim accomplished one miracle even as he died: he swallowed the ninth date of his three circuits before he went to embrace his slave-owner god. He did not allow his blood to wash it away.   (p. 22)

A characteristic feature of Armah's epic style is to open with a short sentence, phrase, or word, followed by a pause, and then a long sentence. This is clearly demonstrated in the Hassan passage. This is the opening paragraph:

> Hassan: Hassan had lived under a terrifying anxiety all his life: the fear that he might chance to live through one day and leave some new carnal pleasure unexamined. This night of nights he ordered six women to prepare themselves for him. They did. When the dawa he had eaten reached his brain what Hassan wanted was one woman, fat and greased with perfumed unctions, under his body for his penis. A second woman — Hassan was not particular as to her size, or indeed as to the size of any of the five apart from the favourite under him — sat in front of his head to one side of the fat one, and welcomed Hassan's tongue and teeth sucking at her genitals.   (p. 23)

The first word, followed by a colon, and the next sentence which is again followed by a colon, give rise to expectation, to heightened expectation. The sensuousness of Hassan is referred to by the words 'carnal pleasure'. The next sentence heightens the effect of these words: 'This night of nights he ordered six women to prepare themselves for him.' The sentence that follows, brief and forceful, is very effective — showing the fulfilment of Hassan's desires and raising the reader's expectation: 'They did'.

On the following page there is a powerful passage which is capable of rousing the reader, of making the reader feel something of the sensuous delight described; a passage which, like others in this chapter, stands on the brink of pornography. The writer exercises no restraint. He chooses that word which shocks, that word that has the maximum effect on the reader. He does not hesitate to tell us that those Arabs who were slain that night 'swam in a viscious paste of shit and their own slimy urine' (p. 24). Such language makes the reader feel how revolting the act is. Armah refers to private parts by those names which one dare not mention in public.

But there is more to come in the section describing Faisal's joys and

sexual activities on this night of nights : 'Faisal sang that night. Laughing
he sang ...' (pp. 22–3). This long paragraph is an example of this talented
writer's lack of consideration for the reader. There is no doubt that here
we have an excellent and powerful description of a gross perversion of
the sex act. It acts as a strong condemnation of both the doer and the
deed. The writer's condemnation of Faisal comes out very clearly in the
tenor of discourse, as is evident in the tone of the third sentence: 'The
words, what were they but a demented Arab praise song to black
bodies?' The emotion that goes into the words 'demented' and 'Arab' is
unmistakable — it is an emotion full of hate and condemnation. As for
the act itself, it is portrayed as being horrifyingly absurd and ugly: a man
having sex with a woman and at the same time another man having sex
with him from behind. It is made more shocking for the reader by the use
of emotionally charged language which many are likely to regard as
indecent and revolting:

> He strode forward at the urgent call and in a moment *was naked*
> *upon his master's back, ploughing the predator's open arsehole while*
> *the master tried to keep his forgetful penis in Azania* ... And Azania
> herself, she slowly, lovingly helped him to slide off her, so gently she
> did not disturb him or the askari *pumping manseed into his Arab*
> *master.*   (p. 23, author's italics)

Because the writer wants us to condemn the act, he uses this kind of
language in order to paint the most vivid picture possible of the horrid
act; but the question is whether the reader is not more shocked by such
evocative description than by the act itself.

Such language would be appropriate if it were the language of the sex
maniacs, the sensuous Arabs. Then it would be in character, the reader
would direct his revulsion at the vulgarity of the Arabs. But what we read
here comes from the mouth of the narrators, the utterers. The young
revolutionaries are in danger of alienating the reader by using language
which veers on the pornographic. The revolutionaries are speaking to
the African public, which has its own taboos and euphemisms in the
sphere of sex. In this connection, I am in complete agreement with the
Marxist critic, Max Adereth, who has said: 'It is one thing to describe sex
without any squeamish disgust, and as *part*, but only part, of human life,
and quite another to aim simply at being crude for no other reason than
the belief that most of us are sure to like it anyway. This cheapens sex and
insults man; it degrades both author and public instead of producing an
uplifting effect, as genuine art usually does.'[5]

Armah's use of evocative language is, of course, not limited to sex and
food. And it is appropriate here to consider whether there are cases in the
book where the reader is shocked not by the language, but by the act
which the language describes.

We can get examples of this in Chapter 5, 'The Dance of Love', where
the young revolutionaries, eleven girls and nine boys, are sold into

slavery. In Chapter 2 we had been shown the cruelties of the destroyers from the desert. In Chapter 5 we are shown the cruelty of the white destroyers from the sea. It is when the twenty young men are on the ship of the white destroyers that they see the full horror of the white man's ways: masses and masses of people are captured and packed into the ship where they are ill-treated, where they meet all manner of disease and death. A good example of the white man's cruelty is the way in which the destroyers, making use of a coloured slavedriver, John, mark each slave with a long hot metal rod. A short passage is worth quoting here to show the power with which Armah describes this most inhuman practice:

> The tall slavedriver pushed the burning iron against the captive's chest where the oil had been smeared and held it there a full moment. The tortured man yelled with pain, once. Smoke rose sharply from the oily flesh then the iron rod was snatched back. Where its end had touched the captive's skin there was now raw, exposed flesh. The skin had come off in two pieces each as long as a middle finger and half as broad.   (p. 118)

Armah makes no attempt to play down the cruelty and inhumanity of slave dealers here. The language is powerful and evocative in its use of strong and expressive words and phrases such as 'yelled with pain', 'the oily flesh', 'raw exposed flesh'. The writer uses such powerful language to terrify and disgust the reader at the inhumanity of those who treat slaves in this way. It is the more powerful because the reader knows that what is described here is not entirely fictitious. Armah is describing vividly and dramatically the cruelty exacted on the African slaves by the whites who bought these human commodities and shipped them off to the Americas to work on sugar plantations.

This passage cannot match the graphic description of the dying slave:

> Now the soft-voiced one held open the slave-driver's mouth and in one movement of amazing speed swung his own exhausted, emaciated, tortured body upward so that the two heads were on a level, his mouth next to the slave-driver's. The slave-driver gave a shuddering jerk, but the grip of the soft-voiced one was strong. The soft-voiced one brought his mouth exactly together with the slavedriver's and then — incredible obedience to will — we saw him with our own eyes bring up all the bile and dead blood from within his body into his mouth, and this mixture he vomited forcefully into the slave-driver's now captive mouth. The slave-driver grew mad with a desperate rage. He tried to tear the sick man's head away from his. In vain. His chest heaved, refusing at first to swallow the deadly vomit from the sick man's mouth. In vain: the sick man's mouth was stuck to the slavedriver's like a nostril to its twin. It was not to be separated by any force outside the sick man himself. The deadly vomit was twice rejected by the

struggling slave-driver. Three times the dying man refused to let it escape harmless on to the ship's wood below. Three times the dying man held the virulent juices, rejected, in his own mouth and throat. Three times with increasing force he pushed them down the slave-driver's reluctant throat. The third time the slave-driver's resistance was broken and the sick man shared death with him, allowing not one drop to escape. Choking, the slave-driver swallowed death with the breath of remaining life. Then he fell to the floor with the soft-voiced one still inseparable from him.   (pp. 131–2)

This is undoubtedly one of the most dramatic scenes in the whole book. The language of this passage is powerful enough to make the reader feel literally sick with disgust. It is the writer's aim to shock. The reticence that we find in Ngugi does not attract Armah. Armah gives words their full force, and he chooses that word and phrase which brings out the desired horrific effect. In the passage just quoted, as in the previous passage, our revulsion is not directed against the language, but against the thing described. To that extent I would argue that these two passages are artistically more successful than the passages dealing with the sexual abnormalities of the Arabs.

Tenor of Discourse

In discussing Armah's use of affective language, we should pay special attention to the tenor of discourse in the novel. Again Chapter 2 serves as a useful starting point. The title itself, 'The Ostentatious Cripples', shows the writer's unfavourable attitude towards the Arabs: those 'predators', those 'beggars' who came trailing wounds on their bodies. As we read further, the contemptuous tone becomes more and more evident. Ramadan is described as 'the predators' season of hypocritical self-denial' (p. 20). In the whole chapter the words 'zombi', 'predators', 'askari', 'Arab', 'orgies', etc. are injected with a feeling which defines in no uncertain terms the author's unfavourable attitude. At times Arabs are described in terms that reduce them to the level of animals:

Noises made by the predators from the desert in their bouts of manic happiness had always been strange to us. This night of nights the noises they made were stranger still. Outside the palace many an askari knew momentary panic wondering if the grunts, the howls, if these shrieks puncturing the air with such accelerating frequency were truly cries of beings possessed with nothing different from joy.   (pp. 20–21)

In this paragraph such words as 'manic happiness', 'grunts', 'howls', 'shrieks' have a degrading and dehumanizing effect. The Arabs are turned into pleasure-loving beasts.

The same contemptuous tone shows itself when Christianity and Islam are referred to:

> We are not stunted in spirit, we are not Europeans, we are not Christians that we should invent fables a child would laugh at and harden our eyes to preach them daylight and deep night as truth. We are not so warped in soul, we are not Arabs, we are not Muslims to fabricate a desert god chanting madness in the wilderness, and call our creature creator.   (p. 3)

When the narrators, the utterers, refer to members of the enemy camp, they do not hesitate to show their contempt for them. This comes out very clearly when there is a roll-call. In Chapter 2, for instance, the names of some of the ostentatious cripples who died in the course of their orgies and sexual absurdities are listed, and this is how we are introduced to the names: 'Hau! Many, so many of the predators from the desert died that beautiful night of blackness. Who asks to hear the mention of the predators' names? Who would hear again the cursed names of the predator chieftains? With which stinking name shall we begin?' (p. 21). Then the names are given: Hussein, Faisal, Mohammed, Hassan, each name followed by a full description of how the owner met his death.

The contemptuous tone is not only reserved for the destroyers. Those of us who were used by the enemy against the people are treated in the same way. Ziblim, the heavy one, is an example of this:

> So among us the ostentatious cripples turned the honoured position of caretakers into plumage for their infirm selves. Which shall we now choose to remember of the many idiocies our tolerance has supported? Shall we remember Ziblim the heavy one, heavy not like a living elephant but like infirm mud, he who wanted every new bride's hymen as his boasting prize, but turned the tears of women into laughter when they found this massive would-be king had not the blood in him for entering the widest open door?   (p. 63)

In the same passage there is a roll-call of those who imposed themselves upon the people, those who chose to be kings against the wishes of the people, those 'cripples' who deserve no mention, no remembrance, but utter contempt:

> Let us make haste to move beyond them and their stinking memory. The smallest arrowpoint they occupy in our thoughts is too much space. But for the terrors flowing from their presence in our midst we should be glad to forget them all — completely, easily. Let us then make haste.
>
> For a cascade of infamy this is: the names and doings of those who from struggling to usurp undeserved positions as caretakers, in the course of generations imposed themselves on a people too

weary of strife to think of halting them. Let us finish speedily with
their mention. The memory of these names is corrosive. Its poison
sears our lips.   (pp. 63–4)

This is a magnificent passage. The intense contempt of kings is
reflected in 'snarl-words' — words of disapproval.[6] There are words and
phrases which are particularly poignant and powerful. The archaic
expression, 'make haste', which is formal and religious in tone, brings out
the desire of the narrators to throw into oblivion the memory of kings,
which memory is said to be 'stinking memory'. So worthless are these
kings that 'the smallest arrowpoint' they occupy in the thoughts of the
'people of the way' is said to be 'too much space' — this is a beautiful and
poignant metaphor. Like 'make haste' the expression 'let us finish
speedily' has a religious ring to it and helps us to feel that the style is
elevated, a style that reflects great seriousness of intent and intensity of
emotion. Such is the intensity of 'the people of the way's' hatred of these
contemptible kings that even the memory of them is 'corrosive'; it is a
poison that cauterizes their lips and makes them wither.

Then follows an impressive list of those monarchical lovers of pomp,
those kings who have imposed themselves on a people 'too weary of strife
to think of halting them':

> Odunton, Bentum, Oko, Krobo, Jebi, Jonto, Sumui, Oburum,
> Ituri, Dube, Mununkum, Esibir, Bonto, Peturi, Topre, Tutu,
> Bonzu, and lately Koranche.   (p. 64)

The rhythm of this litany of names is like that of a monotonous drum. It
may also be observed that the names are not restricted to one region of
Africa. Tutu and Dube, for instance, are Nguni names from southern
Africa. Armah's pan-Africanist attitude is thus expressed in his attack of
monarchical rule. The kings mentioned here need not be identified with
any particular dynasty in Africa and their names are not necessarily
names of kings who have been kings. It is the institution of the monarchy
itself which the writer condemns, for 'The quietest king, the gentlest
leader of the mystified, is criminal beyond the exercise of any
comparison' (p. 64).

An interesting example of Armah's use of tenor of discourse to define
his relationship with a character and what that character stands for
occurs in the passages which portray the personality of Kamuzu.
Kamuzu is a shining example of many post-colonial African rulers who,
empty of any meaningful ideology and slaves to the colonial mentality,
do not hestitate to step into the white man's shoes and perpetrate the
political and social systems inherited from colonial times. As soon as he
gets political power Kamuzu puts himself in the place of the white
destroyer, the colonial governor, and begins to display symbols of power
and pomp. For instance, he has a fantastic flag made: 'a likeness,
supposed to be of himself, standing huge in an attitude of triumph above

adoring heads below' (p. 170). Kamuzu symbolizes the famous emperors and presidents of Africa who glory in praise and lavish titles. The lengthy and high-sounding titles of many rulers in Africa dead and alive, are well known — some of them can fill a whole paragraph — and Armah leaves us in no doubt here that he is satirizing our pompous leaders in post-colonial Africa. In order to blind Kamuzu of their intention to remove quantities of guns and powder from the stone place to their hiding place in the fifth grove, the young revolutionaries, the utterers, feed Kamuzu with the kind of food that appeals to him — resounding appellations:

> What spurious praise names did we not invent to lull Kamuzu's buffoon spirit?
> Osagyefo!
> Kantamanto!
> Kabiyesi!
> Sese!
> Mwenyenguvu!
> Otumfuo!
> Dishonest words are the food of rotten spirits. We filled Kamuzu to bursting with his beloved nourishment.   (p. 171)

But praise names alone are not sufficient for the wild appetite of the pompous one. They must be elaborated if his vain appetite is to be satisfied. It is therefore not sufficient to utter the glorious name of Osagyefo, it is not sufficient to shout Sese. These glorious titles should be clothed in glamorous gowns — each title must be accompanied by songs which praise the uttered title thus:

> Osagyefo, courageous, skilled one who arrives to pulverize the enemy just when the enemy is exulting in imminent victory;
> Mzee, wisdom's own keeper;
> Kabiyesi, leader of men;
> Kantamanto, faithful one who never broke an oath;
> Mtengenezaji, what a multitude of things would remain unrepaired, forever broken were it not for you!
> Katachie, commander supreme!   (p. 172)

There is no room for humour elsewhere in this serious novel, but here we relax and laugh. Though he is levelling a serious criticism against our leaders, Armah certainly wants us to laugh here just as the young revolutionaries would be amused by the ostentatious titles they pile on Kamuzu. In these pages Armah's style comes very close to the light-hearted manner of George Orwell's *Animal Farm*. The praise of Kamuzu is similar to the praise given to Napoleon who, at the height of his glory, was no longer referred to simply as 'Napoleon', but as 'our Leader, Comrade Napoleon'.

The Description of Beauty and Ugliness

Beauty and ugliness are related to the overall theme of the novel. That thing is beautiful which is consonant with 'the way' and which reflects the accepted values of 'the people of the way', and that thing is ugly which is connected with the destroyers and their values. It follows therefore that beauty is not restricted to those things to which the quality of being beautiful is normally ascribed. Beauty thus assumes a wider meaning than it has in ordinary usage. It means, among other things, that which is good, that which is of true value, that which is useful in attaining the goal of those fighting for the rediscovery of 'the way'. Hence 'all beauty is in the creative purposes of our relationships' (p. 206). All that is creative, all that is positive in relation to 'the way' is beautiful. Even relations between people are beautiful. Hence 'The group that knows this and works knowing this, that group itself is a work of beauty, creation's work' (p. 206).

The opposite of creation is destructiveness. Destroyers are destructive and consequently ugly. Hence 'all ugliness is in the destructive aims of the destroyers' arrangements' (p. 206). In describing the destroyers and their deeds, Armah uses language which gives an ugly picture of these people and their deeds. A good example of the ugliness of the destroyers and their ugly deeds has already been given in our discussion of Chapter 2. The sexual abnormalities of the destroyers from the desert are described in terms which bring out a horrid picture of the doer and the deed. The ugliness portrayed in Chapter 2 may be contrasted with the beauty of 'the way' and things connected with 'the way' as described in Chapter 3. This even applies to the physical features of the land belonging to the people of 'the way'. At the end of their epic march, the people of 'the way' are filled with wonder at discovering a part of their land whose beauty is past description. The seers themselves, the utterers, are unable to utter its beauty and are bound to ask:

> With what shall the utterers' tongue stricken with goodness, riven silent with the quiet force of beauty, with which mention shall the tongue of the utterers begin a song of praise whose perfect singers have yet to come?   (p. 56)

This land which is named after the great prophetess herself, Anoa, is a land of mountains, a land of descending slopes, a land of waterfalls, a land of thick forests. It is indeed a wonder, 'a universe of green'. On one level it can be said that the land's geographical position on the African continent cannot be pinpointed since the author seems to indicate that its beauty will be experienced in the future when Africans have discovered 'the way'. It is a land conceived purely in the imagination. On the other hand those from southern Africa may take the description as an accurate reflection of some of the most beautiful spots of the southern African subcontinent: *mosi oa thunya* (known as 'Victoria Falls'), the splendid mountain ranges of South Africa, and the huge forests and green plains of the entire region from the Zambezi to the Limpopo and from the Limpopo to the Atlantic and Indian Oceans. The duiker is of course a southern African antelope and this, coupled with the fact that southern Africa is one of the areas to which the African people came as a result of migrations from the north and north-east, lends some validity to the interpretation.

Here is a passage which shows the sort of language in which the land is described:

> Water hanging clear, water too open to hide the veined rock underneath, water washing pebbles blue and smooth black, yellow like some everlasting offspring of the moon, water washing sand, water flowing to quiet meetings with the swift Esuba, to the broad, quiet Su Tsen, river washing you, Anoa, water washing you.
>
> Land of the duiker, best of animals, attacking none, knowing ways to keep attackers distant, land that should have been perfect for the way, land that will yet be: your praisesong should be woven from the beauty of sounds found only in the future, a beauty springing in its wholeness when the way is found again, Anoa.   (pp. 56–7)

The features of this language to be noted here: the deliberate juxtaposition of 'water' and 'land'; the rhythmical repetition of the word 'water', the cumulative effect of its repetition and the use of postmodifiers which reflect and recreate the magnificence and purity of the river's water. In a style which is itself as clear as the clean waters of a fresh spring, Armah manages to recreate before us a picture of pure and soft-flowing water with such phrases as 'water hanging clear', 'water washing pebbles blue and smooth black', 'water washing sand'.

In the first of these two paragraphs the preponderance of rounded vowels is noticeable, in contrast with the second paragraph where rounded vowels are few and far between. The rhythm of the first paragraph is meant to reflect the rhythm of swift-flowing water. Indeed, as indicated in the second paragraph, the utterers' song is not song enough to describe this beauty, whose sufficiency can only be painted by a voice yet to come. For only when Anoa's prophetic voice has been fulfilled, only when 'the way' as prophesied by Anoa has been found, only then can a voice be found which can match the beauty of the land of clear water, the land of the duiker! For 'the way' itself is a thing of beauty, and beauty can only be realized when all ugliness has been removed, when the ugliness of forces antagonistic to 'the way' has been defeated. One is reminded of the title of Armah's first novel, *The Beautyful Ones Are Not Yet Born*. Even here we are told that those are not yet born who can give a full picture of the beauty of this land of the 'people of the way', a land yet to be born. But in this passage we are given hope that the beautiful ones *will* be born, for this is a land 'that will yet be', a land whose praisesong 'should be woven from the beauty of sounds found only in the future'. But the truth of the matter is that in these words, by this same utterance, Armah has created a song that can hardly be surpassed by other voices, be they voices of the past or of the present or of the future.

The contradiction between beauty and ugliness is symbolized in the contrast between the two colours, white and black. White is the colour of the destroyers and therefore all white things are ugly, and all ugly things are associated with the colour white. This contradiction can be clearly demonstrated by citing the following passage, which describes a time of hardship in the history of 'the people of the way':

> Those seasons fords were things to laugh at. For six seasons babies did not fear to crawl along the river-bed itself. The water was so far we forgot the blackness of its flowing. The clouds left in the sky were streaky, wispy, barren, white. It has come down that the men — cursed the tyranny of belly and tongue — were most concerned to have water enought to mix their ahey in, and then they sat through moistureless afternoons season after season consuming stored supplies, staring up at the clear white skies, muttering mutual incoherencies about the beauty of such skies — how often the unconnected eye finds beauty in death — while the women looked at the same whiteness, saw famine where the men saw beauty, and grew frightened for our people.   (p. 11)

Here water is associated with life, therefore it is given the colour black. Rainless clouds are symbols of the absence of the life-giving force, rain, and so they are white and their white colour is associated with death. Earlier in the chapter we are told that 'the disease of death' is 'the white road' (p. 8). Those of us who have lost 'the way' will associate white things with beauty, while those faithful to 'the way', like the women in the passage quoted above, can see the ugliness of the white colour.

White has been traditionally associated with good values among the English and other European races, and black with everything bad and ugly. Sins are black, Satan is black, while virginity, purity and innocence are associated with white. The English poet, William Blake, wrote the well-known poem, 'The Little Black Boy', where he depicts a black boy feeling guilty for being black and hoping to be white like an English child when he is in heaven. The little English boy, who is white, is likened to an angel, while the black boy associates his black colour with darkness and absence of light. Black is therefore negative because it reflects the absence of something positive — light. This is the first stanza of the poem:

> My mother bore me in the southern wild,
> and I am black, but O! my soul is white;
> White as an angel is the English child,
> But I am black, as if bereav'd of light.   *William Blake*

In Armah, the 'black is beautiful' and 'white is ugly' theme is also evident in the writer's description of white and black characters. A good example of how white carries negative connotations is in the description of Bentum's white wife:

> Now from the gate to the falling came first an apparition exactly like a ghost: a pale white woman in white clothes moving with a disjointed, severe, jerky walk, like a profoundly discontented walker. Her walk was like that of a beginning stiltwalker, but an angry beginner. Her face was squeezed in a severe frown that had formed three permanent vertical creases on her lower forehead in the space between her eyes. She had no eyebrows. Eyelashes she had, but they were hard to discern, being white and therefore merging into the pallor of her face. On her head she wore a white hat. As she came in there was space before her, space to her left and right, space behind her: her figure seemed the shape itself of loneliness. It seemed impossible that she could ever be together with any other being.   (p. 119)

Small wonder that Abena, that black paragon of beauty, should exclaim: 'So this white ghost was to have been my rival wife' (p. 120).

Now contrast the ugliness of this 'white phantom' with the beauty of Idawa, the black woman who was the object of Koranche's lust:

> There was a woman. Idawa was her name. There are not many born with every generation of whom it may be said they have a beauty needing no counterpointing blemish to make its wonder clear. The best moulded face may lead the admiring eye in the end down to a pair of lumpen legs. The slenderest neck may sit incongruous on a bloated bosom. Idawa had a beauty with no such disappointment in it. Seen from a distance her shape in motion told the looker here was co-ordination free, unforced. From the hair on her head to the last of her toes there was nothing wasted in her shaping. And her colour: that must have come uninterfered with from night's own blackness.   (pp. 69–70)

But Armah is not only concerned with physical beauty which is mere surface beauty. Physical beauty must be complemented by and indeed be a reflection of a more profound beauty — internal beauty. Hence Idawa's beauty goes much deeper than what men see with the naked eye:

> Men may crave closeness to such physical beauty and still be forgiven even if their loved one has no suspicion of an answering beauty in her soul. But Idawa's surface beauty, perfect as it was, was nothing beside her other, profounder beauties: the beauty of her heart, the way she was with people, the way she was with everything she came in contact with; and the beauty of her mind, the clarity with which she moved past the lying surfaces people held in front of themselves, past the lying surfaces of the

things of this world set against our way, to reach judgments
holding to essences, free from the superficies.   (p. 70)

The beauty of the body then should be complemented by the beauty of
heart and mind — a perfect co-ordination of the physical, the spiritual
and the intellectual in man and woman.

We notice here that the language is free from words with unpleasant
connotations. It is a language that calls forth no sense of revulsion and is
far from the absurdities and vulgarities of the ostentatious cripples from
the desert, far from the rotten spirits and insatiate desires of those who
came trailing wounds on their bodies.

Conclusion

The account presented here does not claim to do complete justice to this
great novel. Apart from the fact that other critics may respond quite
differently to some aspects of the novel, there are areas which need a
much closer attention than is possible here. These areas include the
writer's use of poetic devices, for instance, rhythm and metre; the
relationship between the novel and oral tradition; symbolism; the
significance of the names; and, finally, the extent to which the events
described in the book correlate with actual facts in African history.
Someone who knows Armah's mother tongue and Swahili (in which he is
fluent) is probably better qualified to deal with some of these problems.

Since the main concern of my analysis is with language, I shall try to
state very briefly some of the significant aspects not discussed so far. One
is that like Achebe, Tutuola and Okara, Armah is very much concerned
about how to use English in a way that presents an African point of view.
But Armah does so in a very different way from these other writers. We
notice, for instance, that he does not bombard the reader with African
proverbs as Achebe does, nor does he make us feel that we are reading a
translation from an African language. His use of the English language,
putting aside the tenor of discourse and the writer's handling of the
language of sex, is likely to appeal to any English reader as fully as it does
to African readers. The rhythms which are no doubt based on the ancient
rhythms of Africa, are nevertheless perfectly consonant with the rhythms
of the English language. The language is English, but it is English that
has been decolonized.

The decolonization of the language is a very important feature of the
book. Using the English language, Armah presents an African
viewpoint. We notice, for instance, that in handling directions and time,
Armah does not reflect European concepts. Time is measured in terms of
'seasons' and 'moons', not 'years' and 'months'. The directions referred to
in the book are the west and the east, and these are called 'the falling' and
'the rising'. Such expressions are equivalent to those of my own language,
Shona, where, the west is *madokero* 'the setting direction' and the east

mabvazuva 'the direction from which the sun comes'. Generally there is a refusal on the part of 'the people of the way' to call things after the white man's fashion, and so the castle is referred to as 'the stone place', a master or expert is called a 'fundi', a Swahili word.

Further, the writer injects into his writing what he considers to be an African view of westerners and Arabs. By his special use of words and expressions like 'ostentatious cripples', 'predators', 'destroyers', 'slave-owning god', and so on. Armah is creating an African world view which parallels and contrasts with that of Europeans and Arabs who call us natives, primitive people, heathens, kaffirs, tribes. Thus things African are given positive qualities by the way such words and expressions as 'the way', 'our way', 'remembrance', 'black', are surrounded with an aura of beauty and admiration. Conversely all things white and Arab carry negative connotations.

Armah also does something to the English language which is not simply Africanization or decolonization. He may be said to want to rationalize the English language by giving a consistent form to nouns. Thus we find a fairly frequent use of words ending in *er*, for instance, smiler, looker, offerer, giver, utterer, hearer, rememberer, preparers, and so on.

Two Thousand Seasons is very readable and persuasive. Compelling power is considerable in those passages where we identify with characters, for example, when Abena is dancing before the king who wants her to choose his son, Bentum, renamed Bradford George, for a husband. The audience identifies with Abena and dislikes Bentum, and so we are held in suspense as we want to see what choice she will make. Or again when Isanusi is fighting with the mercenary sent to murder him in the grove, we are held in suspense, anxious to see Isanusi escape with his life; likewise in the graphic description of the fight between John, the half-black and half-white slave-driver, and the dying man with a decomposing body. We also feel the compelling power of the book when following the heroic march of the people of the way through the bog.

There are many memorable passages in the book. Apart from those just cited there is the passage describing the marking of the slaves with the hot iron rod. That passage's shrieking cruelty makes it difficult to forget.

Taking the book as a whole we can correctly say that what most sustains the reader's interest is the language: its haunting rhythms, its enchanting quality, its evocative power, its mangificence, its readability. If at times one feels that the writer is being unneccessarily wordy and repetitious, that more is said than necessary, there is nevertheless no doubt that the writer's achievement in using language is very great indeed. In a novel where the role of character and plot is minimal, and in such a long novel, the reader could easily get bored and throw the book away were it not for the power of the incantatory and elevated language.

The writer's linguistic choices are in the most part appropriate and admirable. The exception is the language he uses to write about sexual depravity. For some readers this spoils the splendour of the book. The style of *Two Thousand Seasons* is indeed sublime, but it is a sublimity that is marred by vulgarity and this, in my opinion, is regrettable, for it means that the reader is left with mixed feelings, one of admiration and another of disappointment.

Be that as it may, *Two Thousand Seasons* is a great epic. The amount of material covered and the vision given to the African people are fantastic and admirable. There is nothing so far written in African fiction to surpass its excellence of language, its epic splendour, its intense moral earnestness. It is a novel which deserves the attention of all African readers.

Notes

1 See D. T. Niane, *Sundiata: An Epic of Old Mali*, p. 12.
2 For a definition of the term 'parallelism' see Geoffrey Leech, *A Linguistic Guide to English Poetry*, p. 79.
3 *Encyclopedia Americana*, Vol. XIX.
4 See T. S. Dorsch, *Classical Literary Criticism*, p. 108.
5 See David Craig, *Marxists on Literature*, p. 452.
6 S. I. Hayakawa uses the term 'snarl-words' to denote words of disapproval. See *Language in Thought and Action*, Chapter 3.

Bibliography

Achebe, C. (1974 2nd edition) *Arrow of God*, London, Heinemann African Writers Series.

Achebe, C. (1975) *Morning Yet on Creation Day*, London, Heinemann Educational Books.

Armah, A. K. (1979) *Two Thousand Seasons*, London, Heinemann African Writers Series.

Armah, A. K. (1977) 'Larsony or Fiction as Criticism of Fiction', *New Classic*, No. 4.

Blake, W. (1958) *William Blake*, J. Bronowski (ed.), Harmondsworth, Penguin.

Boulton, M. (1975) *The Anatomy of the Novel*, London, Routledge & Kegan Paul.

Bradbury, M. (1969) *What is a Novel?* London, Edward Arnold.

Bradbury, M. (1973) *Possibilities*, Oxford, Oxford University Press.

Bradbury, M. and Palmer, D. (eds) (1970) Stratford-upon-Avon Studies 12: *Contemporary Criticism*, London, Edward Arnold.

Chapman, R. (1973) *Linguistics and Literature: An Introduction to Literary Stylistics*, London, Edward Arnold.

Chukwukere, B. I. (1969) 'The Problem of Language in African Creative Writing' in *African Literature Today*, No. 3, London, Heinemann Educational Books.

Collins, Fontana Books (1973) The Revised Standard Version Common Bible.

Collins, H. R. (1969) *Amos Tutuola*, New York, Twayne Publishers, Inc.

Craig, D. (1975) (ed.) *Marxists on Literature*, Harmondsworth, Penguin.

Crane, R. (1953) *The Languages of Criticism and the Structure of Poetry*, Toronto, University of Toronto Press.

Crystal, D. and Davy, D. (1969) *Investigating English Style*, Harlow, Longman.

Dathorne, O. R. (1975) *African Literature in the Twentieth Century*, London, Heinemann Educational Books.

Davis, R. M. (1969) *The Novel: Modern Essays in Criticism*, Englewood Cliffs NJ, Prentice-Hall, Inc.

Dorsch, T. S. (ed.) (1965) *Classical Literary Criticism*, Harmondsworth, Penguin.

Eagleton, T. (1976) *Marxism and Literary Criticism*, London, Methuen & Co. Ltd.

Eliot, T. S. (1920) *The Sacred Wood*, London, Methuen (University Paperbacks), 1960, Reprinted 1969.

Enkvist, N., Spencer, J. and Gregory, M. (1964) *Linguistics and Style*, Oxford, Oxford University Press.

Fischer, E. (1959) *The Necessity of Art: A Marxist Approach*, Dresden, Verlag der Kunst; Harmondsworth, Penguin (1963).

Fowler, R. (ed.) (1966) *Essays on Style and Language*, London, Routledge & Kegan Paul.

Fowler, R. (ed.) (1971) *The Languages of Literature*, London, Routledge & Kegan Paul.

Fowler, R. (ed.) (1977) *Linguistics and the Novel*, London, Methuen & Co. Ltd.

Freeman, D. C. (1970) *An Approach to the Study of Style*, New York, Holt, Rinehart and Winston.

Freeman, D. C. (1970) *Linguistics and Literary Style*, New York, Holt, Rinehart and Winston.

Gordimer, N. (1973) *The Black Interpreters*, Johannesburg, Spro-Cas/Ravan Press.

Hardy, B. (1964, 1971) *The Appropriate Form*, London, The Athlone Press.

Hayakawa, S. I. (1964, 2nd edition) *Language in Thought and Action*, London, George Allen & Unwin.

Jones, E. D. (1973a) *The Writing of Wole Soyinka*, London, Heinemann Educational Books.

Jones, E. D. (1973b) 'Wole Soyinka: Critical Approaches' in E. Wright *The Critical Evaluation of African Literature*.

Kane, T. S. and Peters, L. J. (1969 3rd edition) *Writing Prose: Techniques and Purposes*, Oxford, Oxford University Press.

King, B. (1971) *Introduction to Nigerian Literature*, Lagos, University of Lagos; London, Evans Brothers, Ltd.

Kronenfeld, J. Z. (1975) 'The "Communalist" African and the "Individualistic" Westerner: Some Comments on Misleading Generalizations in Western Criticism of Soyinka and Achebe', *Research in African Literatures*, Vol. 6, No. 2.

Larson, C. R. (1971) *The Emergence of African Fiction*, Bloomington, Indiana University Press.

Leech, G. N. (1969) *A Linguistic Guide to English Poetry*, Harlow, Longman.

Lichtheim, M. (1975) *Ancient Egyptian Literature*, Vol. 1, Berkeley, University of California Press.

Lindfors, B. (1968) 'The Palm Oil With Which Achebe's Words Are Eaten', *African Literature Today*, No. 1, London, Heinemann Educational Books.

Lodge, D. (1966) *Language of Fiction*, London, Routledge & Kegan Paul.

Lukács, G. (1962) *The Historical Novel*, London, The Merlin Press.

Lukács, G. (1972) *Studies in European Realism*, London, The Merlin Press.

Macebuh, S. (1974) 'African Aesthetics in Traditional African Art', *Okike*, No. 5.

Macksey, R. and Donato, E. (eds) (1970) *The Languages of Criticism and the Sciences of Man*, Baltimore, Johns Hopkins University Press.

Milton, J. (1966) *Poetical Works*, Douglas Bush (ed.), Oxford, Oxford University Press.

Modisane, B. (1962) 'African Writers' Summit', *Transition*, Vol. 2, No. 5.

Moore, G. (ed.) (1965) *African Literature and the Universities*, Ibadan, Ibadan University Press.

Mphahlele, E. (1963) 'African Literature and Universities', *Transition*, Vol. 4, No. 10.

Ngara, E. A. (1974a) *The Significance of Time and Motion in the Poetry of T. S. Eliot* — with Special Reference to the Teaching of Eliot in Rhodesia. M.Phil thesis, London University.

Ngara, E. A. (1974b) 'A Redefinition of the Role of the English Language in African Universities', *Bulletin of the Association of African Universities*, Vol. 1, No. 2.

Ngugi wa Thiong'o (1975 edition) *A Grain of Wheat*, London, Heinemann African Writers Series.

Niane, D. T. (1965) *Sundiata: An Epic of Old Mali*, Harlow, Longman.

Nowottny, W. (1965) *The Language Poets Use*, London, The Athlone Press.

Obiechina, E. N. (1972) 'Art and Artifice in Okara's *The Voice*', *Okike*, Vol. 1, No. 3.

Obiechina, E. N. (1975) *Culture, Tradition and Society in the West African Novel*, Cambridge, Cambridge University Press.

Ogumba, O. (1970) 'The Traditional Content of the Plays of Wole Soyinka', *African Literature Today*, No. 4, London, Heinemann Educational Books.

Okara, G. (1963) 'African Speech — English Words', *Transition*, Vol. 3, No. 10.

Okara, G. (1970) *The Voice*, London, Heinemann African Writers Series.

Olney, J. (1973) *Tell me Africa: An Approach to African Literature*, Princeton, Princeton University Press.

Orwell, G. (1945) *Animal Farm*, Harmondsworth, Penguin.

Palmer, E. (1972) *An Introduction to the African Novel*, London, Heinemann Educational Books.

Povey, J. (1970) 'Styles and Themes in the African Novel in English', *English Studies in Africa*, Vol. 13, No. 1.

Ravenscroft, A. (1969) 'Introduction' to *The Voice*, in Okara, 1970.

Richards, I. A. (1970 edition) *Principles of Literary Criticism*, London, Routledge & Kegan Paul, 1960, Reprinted 1970.

Ruhumbika, G. (1969) *Village in Uhuru*, Harlow, Longman.

Scholes, R. and Kellog, R. (1966) *The Nature of Narrative*, Oxford, Oxford University Press.

Searle, C. (1972) *The Forsaken Lover: White Words and Black People*, London, Routledge & Kegan Paul.

Skeat, W. W. (1869) *Langland's Vision of Piers the Plowman*, Oxford, Oxford University Press.

Soyinka, W. (1973) *Season of Anomy*, London, Rex Collings.

Spencer, J. and Gregory, M. J. (1970) 'An Approach to the Study of Style' in D. C. Freeman (ed.) *Linguistics and Literary Style*.

Tejani, B. (1973) 'Creative Freedom and Critical Functions in African Literature', in C. L. Wanjala, 1973.

Tibble, A. (ed.) (1965) *African–English Literature*, London, Peter Owen.

Tsodzo, T. K. (1972) *Pafunge*, Salisbury, Longman Publishers (PVT).

Vincent, T. (1974) 'Designing a Course in African Literature', *Research in African Literatures*, Vol. 5, No. 1.

Volosinov, V. N. (1973) *Marxism and the Philosophy of Language*, translated by Matejka & Titunic, New York, Seminar Press.

Wali, O. (1963) 'The Dead End of African Literature?' *Transition*, Vol. 3, No. 10.

Wanjala, C. L. (ed.) (1973) *Standpoints on African Literature*, Nairobi, East African Literature Bureau.

Wauthier, C. (1966) *The Literature and Thought of Modern Africa*, London, Pall Mall Press and (1978) Heinemann Educational Books.

Wellek, R. and Warren, A. (1963) *Theory of Literature*, Harmondsworth, Penguin.

Wright, E. (ed.) (1973) *The Critical Evaluation of African Literature*, London, Heinemann Educational Books.

Index